THE
"FALLEN WESTERN STAR" WARS

Also by Jack Foley

Criticism

Inciting Big Joy: A Monograph on James Broughton
"O Her Blackness Sparkles!" The Life and Times of the
	Batman Art Gallery
O Powerful Western Star: Poetry and Art in California
Foley's Books: California Rebels, Beats, and Radicals

Poetry

Letters/Lights—Words for Adelle
Gershwin
Adrift
Exiles
New Poetry from California: Dead / Requiem
	(with Ivan Argüelles)
Advice to the Lovelorn
Saint James (with Ivan Argüelles)
Some Songs by Georges Brassens

THE
"FALLEN WESTERN STAR"
WARS

A Debate About
Literary California

EDITED BY JACK FOLEY

BOOKS

Grateful acknowledgment is made to the print and online magazines in which some of these essays first appeared: *The Alsop Review*, *For Poetry*, *The Hungry Mind Review*, *Poetry Flash*, *The Press Democrat* and *San Francisco Magazine*.

Cover photograph: Gene Anthony
Author photograph: Adelle Foley
Painting of author (in author photograph): Anthony Holdsworth
Design: DuFlon Design, Berkeley, CA
Composition: Archetype Typography, Berkeley, CA

Published by Scarlet Tanager Books
P.O. Box 20906
Oakland, CA 94620
www.scarlettanager.com

Library of Congress Cataloging-in-Publication Data

The "Fallen Western Star" wars : a debate about literary California /
edited by Jack Foley
       p. cm.
   ISBN 0-9670224-4-4 (alk. paper)
   1. American literature—California—San Francisco Bay Area—History
and criticism. 2. Criticism—California—San Francisco Bay
Area—History. 3. American literature—West (U.S.)—History and
criticism. 4. American literature—California—History and criticism.
5. San Francisco Bay Area (Calif.)—Intellectual life. 6. San
Francisco Bay Area (Calif.)—In literature. 7. West
(U.S.)—Intellectual life. 8. California—Intellectual life. 9. West
(U.S.)—In literature. 10. California—In literature. I. Foley, Jack, 1940-
   PS285.S3 F35 2001
   810.9'97946—dc21
                                                    2001002622

In principle, I believe that literature—both creative and critical—is a conversation. Having had my say in an essay or a poem, I must allow the readers to have their responses, be they favorable, unfavorable, or mixed. Reading the hundreds of printed responses to "Can Poetry Matter?" . . . taught me that readers often need to put my writing to ends important to themselves even if they do not (to my mind at least) directly bear on the issues as I stated them. To be used, I realized, often meant to be misused in ways that the reader felt were important or productive. I also feel that once a work is published, I simply become another reader—and one just as likely to misread my own work.

—Dana Gioia

CONTENTS

Jack Foley

PREFACE

Coleridge is . . . distinguishing between [the] personal need to see the strong, self-contained mind as the creator of its own values and the general modes of writing and reading great poetry—which requires a literate and thoughtful public and a poet who knows how to communicate with other minds and needs to do it. . . .
> —A.S. Byatt, *Unruly Times: Wordsworth and Coleridge in Their Time*

"I'm teaching my students to publish in New York."
> —A teacher at New College of California

In the Winter 1999-2000 issue of the *Hungry Mind Review* (now the *Ruminator Review*) poet-critic Dana Gioia published an article, "Fallen Western Star," on the San Francisco Bay Area as a literary region. Bart Schneider, editor of *The Hungry Mind Review*, explained that he had asked Gioia "to write an essay about the literary life of his region, and he delivered so provocative and thorough a piece that I asked eight other writers from around the country to report on the literary doings in their regions."

Subtitled "The Decline of San Francisco as a Literary Region," Gioia's 9,000-word historical/theoretical article is not easy to characterize: its strength lies partly in the wide range of its insights. Yet the general argument is clear. "In 1899," writes Gioia, "San Francisco was a major literary center": it "represented a bohemian and democratic alternative to the East Coast's genteel and academic traditions. Its best writers not only added to American literature, they transformed it." Now, however, "San Francisco no longer ranks as an influential literary center," though "the demise of its cultural power does not result from a paucity of talent": "What San Francisco—and by extension all West Coast cities—lacks is a vital and complete literary milieu." In 1899 the city boasted "a diverse literary ecosystem of newspapers, magazines, publishers, and theaters that not only fostered but also promoted local talent." Today, he sighs, "the publishers have mostly moved to New York"; the "dynamic milieu" of a hundred years ago has been replaced by pockets of activity which may give the writer "privacy" but deprive him of "the considerable intellectual energy of social interaction": "As Bay Area intellectual life spread out and suburbanized, bohemia slowly broke up." At this point, Gioia argues—despite the many talented writers living in the area— San Francisco has become a "museum city," a place which remains "fixated in its last moment of natural literary glory—the Beat movement of the 1950s."

Gioia's article grew partially out of the introduction he had written to my book, O Powerful Western Star (Pantograph Press, 2000), which is, among other things, a celebration of the San Francisco literary region. The title of Gioia's article is a reference to the line in Walt Whitman's "When Lilacs Last in the Dooryard Bloom'd" which gave me my title, and his essay begins with an explicit reference to my book.

Flying in the face of the popular conception of San Francisco as a wonderful place for writers—a conception which this tourist-oriented city is eager to foster—Gioia's challenging piece immediately aroused interest. Like the author's earlier and equally challenging "Can Poetry Matter?" [*The Atlantic Monthly*, vol. 267, no. 5, May, 1991; reprinted in *Can Poetry Matter?: Essays on Poetry and American Culture* (Graywolf Press, 1992)], "Fallen Western Star" had its passionate adherents. Kevin Berger, a lifelong Bay Area resident and senior editor of *San Francisco Magazine*—for which Gioia writes a regular column—requested a summary of the piece. BBC radio recorded a shortened version of the article for broadcast in Europe. I recorded Gioia reading the piece in its entirety for my KPFA radio show, *Cover to Cover*. Poet and anthologist David Mason; Jacqueline J. Marcus, editor of the online magazine *For Poetry*; Michael Lind, Washington editor of *Harper's*; and Scott Timberg of the *LA New Times* all greeted the article as a breath of fresh air—a moment of refreshing honesty in the midst of a situation which had grown increasingly murky.

Controversy began almost at once. Howard Junker, editor of *ZYZZYVA*, sent a blistering letter to *The Hungry Mind Review*. Jonah Raskin, chair of the Communications Department at Sonoma State University, also responded to Gioia's article, though Raskin's tone was considerably milder than Junker's. Raskin's piece, "Local Literary Scene Is Worth Celebrating," appeared in *The Press Democrat* on Wednesday, December 15, 1999.

The most detailed response to Dana Gioia's article was written by Richard Silberg, respected critic and Associate Editor of *Poetry Flash*. It was titled "On 'Fallen Western Star': Dana Gioia Stirs It Up in the *Hungry Mind Review*," and it was published in *Poetry Flash*, Number 285, May-June 2000. Silberg makes a number of valuable points. My response to his piece, "The Black Hole of Criticism: Richard Silberg on Dana Gioia's 'Fallen Western Star,'" appeared in the following issue, Number 286, September-October 2000, along with Silberg's response to what I had written. Jacqueline Marcus, David Mason and Scott Timberg also produced pieces dealing with "Fallen Western Star." I was interviewed about the subject on *Dancing Bear's Poetry Program*, KKUP, Cupertino in September 2000, and a transcription of the broadcast appeared in my column, "Foley's Books," in *The Alsop Review* (www.alsopreview.com).

All these pieces—including Gioia's original essay—appear in this book. Though Gioia's essay deals with literature in general—prose as well as poetry—the debate has tended to center on poetry.

Is the controversy over "Fallen Western Star" a tempest in a tea-pot—Californians arguing over regional trivialities—or are larger issues involved? Gioia, like Scott Timberg a native Californian, asks,

> Is urban culture still a viable reality for American cities outside the Northeast corridor? Or is some new social means of concentrating human talent needed? Is the delocalized and disembodied cyberspace of the Internet the American writer's only alternative to New York? These questions are especially pressing in the West where huge distances separate urban areas and the major cities often lack identifiable centers. Does the concept of Western literature still have meaning as a collective entity, or does it exist only as a remote abstraction in the work of isolated individual writers?
>
> These are not abstract issues to California writers. Any serious literary artist in California, at least one writing in English, feels the competing claims of language and experience . . . Our seasons, climate, landscape, wildlife, and history are alien to the world views of both England and New England. The world looks and feels different in California from the way it does in either York or New York—not only the natural landscape but also the urban one . . . The deepest European roots are Latin and Catholic, not Anglo-Saxon and Puritan. Asia and Latin America are omnipresent influences. There is no use listening for a nightingale among the scrub oaks and chaparral. Our challenge is not only to find the right words to describe our new and complex experience but also to discover the right images, myths, concepts, and characters. For us, this is an essential task, and one impossible to have done elsewhere. We must describe a reality that has never been fully captured in English.

"Human existence," Gioia's article reminds us, "is local." Whatever the marvelous possibilities of the Internet—and they are many—the air we breathe, the climate we take in (intellectual as well as physical) is always *right here, right now*. What effect does that have upon us? What does it mean to say, as so many poets have, that poetry comes from the "body"? How does a "disembodied" medium like the Internet—like print, for that matter—serve poetry? Beyond this, what California poets are "important"? Which poets will "live"?

Richard Silberg's or Howard Junker's list of "important" California poets would be very different from Dana Gioia's. As all these writers know, the question is not merely a matter of taste but of history. Richard Silberg takes the position that the Bay Area is indeed "a vital, influential poetry scene": i.e., it's doing just fine. Similarly, Howard Junker writes, "A lot of things suck in the Bay Area—the Warriors, the 49ers, the theater, the layout of the new Main Library, the collection of the Museum of Modern Art, bagels . . . but the literary scene does not." Gioia's criticisms are taken by both men to be an insult to the honor of the region, and they are quick to defend the Bay Area from such ungallant, upstart opinions.

Gioia's criticism of the Bay Area's poetry scene in turn arises partly out of his thrust towards "a reality that has never been fully captured in English": it is a deliberate movement towards a possible future. But a new future means a redefinition of the past, a new naming of predecessors. Interestingly, three distinguished California writers who are extremely important to Dana Gioia—Weldon Kees, Yvor Winters, and Janet Lewis—are nowhere to be found in James D. Hart's supposedly "comprehensive" *A Companion to California* (Oxford University Press, 1978).

The reader will have to decide who is right in all this. The evidence is here. Focusing on issues such as the relationship of the body to communications media, localism versus cyberspace, the possibilities of a resurgence of regional writing, the question of what constitutes a literary community, the question of what makes for great poetry, the debate enunciated here is surely a defining moment not only of California literature but of contemporary American literature—of writing itself. Like Coleridge, Gioia recognizes "the strong, self-contained mind as the creator of its own values." California literature is filled with such rugged individualists. But, like Coleridge, Gioia also insists upon "the general modes of writing and reading great poetry—which requires a literate and thoughtful public and a poet who knows how to communicate with other minds and needs to do it."

These are the questions. The answers are not, finally, in our power to give. "Fallen Western Star" takes us into the fray.

Dana Gioia

FALLEN WESTERN STAR

The Decline of San Francisco as a Literary Region

I.

O Powerful Western Star
    —Title of Jack Foley's critical book on
    Bay Area culture (2000)

In 1899 San Francisco was a major literary center—a city where influential new trends emerged and young writers achieved national reputations. Not only was the Bay Area noted for developing its local talent, true originals like Jack London, Bret Harte, Edwin Markham, Lincoln Steffens, and Frank Norris; it had also long attracted ambitious newcomers from elsewhere like Mark Twain and Ambrose Bierce. What better place was there in America to serve a literary apprenticeship than this raw but strangely sophisticated boomtown where even a stagecoach robber like Black Bart wrote poetry? Northern California also drew foreign literati, most notably Robert Louis Stevenson and John Muir, and the region's climate—both meteorological and intellectual—attracted literary invalids like the consumptive Stevenson and the post-breakdown Charlotte Perkins Gilman.

In the days before television and radio, national taste and opinion were not yet created exclusively in broadcast capitals like New York and Los Angeles. Strong city newspapers commanded national attention. A brilliant local journalist like Bierce at the *San Francisco Examiner* exercised immense influence (just as a little later H. L. Mencken would shape political and cultural opinion from the *Baltimore Sun*). San Francisco, which was then the center of William Randolph Hearst's newspaper empire and home to dozens of other journals, helped set the agenda of American literature.

What emerged was a distinctive local literature that reflected San Francisco's unique geography, history, and population. The literature of this Gold Rush seaport was innovative, irreverent, populist, and yet oddly international—notably different from the writing of other American literary centers of the era like Boston, New York, Chicago, and Philadelphia. No one would confuse a page of Frank Norris or Jack London with one by William Dean Howells or Edith Wharton. San Francisco represented a bohemian and democratic alternative to the East Coast's genteel and academic traditions. Its best writers not only added to American literature, they transformed it. American Naturalism, for example, was largely the creation of San Francisco and Chicago newspaper-trained novelists. London was America's first significant working-class writer. Japanese-born Yone Noguchi became the first Asian-American author of note. These writers would not have emerged in Boston or Baltimore.

One anecdote will suffice to demonstrate both the power and personality of *fin de siècle* San Franciscan literary culture. On January 15, 1899 Edwin Markham, a forty-seven-year-old Oakland high school teacher, published "The Man with the Hoe" in the *San Francisco Examiner*. Based on the celebrated Jean-François Millet painting, which had recently been exhibited in San Francisco, this forty-nine-line blank verse poem dramatized the perpetual burden of the oppressed worker and condemned the treatment of labor. Newspapers were the Internet of the nineteenth century—a decentralized information system—and "The Man with the Hoe" was reprinted from paper to paper first across the United States and then abroad. Translated into more than forty languages, it was eventually republished in 10,000 newspapers and magazines. In the early twentieth century there was no more famous American poem than Markham's. The poet became an international celebrity, and the poem served as a literary call to arms for the labor movement—all of which began with the *San Francisco Examiner*.

The popular sentiment was not misplaced. One hundred years later "The Man with the Hoe" remains an extraordinary poem—vivid, forceful, compressed, and deeply moving. Although the poem still has many readers, it rarely appears in current anthologies, so it may help to quote a few lines to convey its particular quality. After an ironic epigraph from *Genesis*, "God made man in His own image . . ." Markham begins with Millet's pathetic image of a wretched laborer bent over a hoe:

> Bowed by the weight of centuries he leans
> Upon his hoe and gazes on the ground,
> The emptiness of ages in his face,
> And on his back the burden of the world.

Slowly and passionately the poet builds to his final stanza—an apocalyptic vision of the future when the worker's anger, resentment, and desire are unleashed. No American poet—and especially no poet of the Gilded Age—provided a truer prophecy of the bitter social turmoil of the early twentieth century:

> O masters, lord and rulers in all lands,
> How will the future reckon with this man?
> How answer his brute question in that hour
> When whirlwinds of rebellion shake all shores?
> How will it be with kingdoms and with kings—
> With those who shaped him to the thing he is—
> When this dumb Terror shall rise to judge the world,
> After the silence of the centuries?

Although no one ever cites it as such, Markham's "The Man with the Hoe" was and remains the quintessential Bay Area poem—a representative work for the best that would follow over the next century. It offers a populist and progressive but unillusioned view of existence. It dramatizes the lone individual against the system without idealizing the protagonist into an unrealistically noble figure. The poem's perspective dares to take the long view of human history and does not shy away from suggesting universals. The style is both visionary and naturalistic. The concerns are moral and political. The manner of the poem is quite contemporary for the late Victorian era, and yet its modernity is deeply rooted in the past. The poetic and ideological allegiances are thoroughly cosmopolitan, as much international as American. Finally, the poem is conceived for oral delivery—it is accessible, dramatic, and auditory. These same qualities can be found, *mutatis mutandis*, in later Northern Californian poets including such otherwise diverse figures as Robinson Jeffers, Kenneth Rexroth, Yvor Winters, Allen Ginsberg, Robert Duncan, William Everson, Gary Snyder, Josephine Miles, Lawrence Ferlinghetti, and Thom Gunn. And these qualities link the poets to the populist outsider politics native to the Bay Area from Lincoln Steffens and Upton Sinclair through Eric Hoffer and Jerry Brown.

Although extremely different in their aesthetics, these poets share crucial assumptions that might best be called Populist Modernism. They explored new styles and subjects without ever deliberately limiting their work to a coterie audience of literati. Compare a poem by Jeffers or Ginsberg to one by Wallace Stevens or Hart Crane, and the stubbornly public nature of Northern California poetry becomes obvious. Even a New Critical modernist and academic formalist like Winters, an early champion of Crane and Stevens, developed a poetic style that was accessible, realistic, and auditory. (The cerebral Winters once spent a year preparing and publishing the defense of a local man unjustly convicted and condemned to death for murder. *The Case of David Lamson* in 1934 resulted in overturning the conviction—hardly the sort of scholarly project any other New Critic would have undertaken.) Poetry was not conceived as a self-enclosed text for private meditation but as a direct address to an audience. There is an essential line of development that stretches from "The Man with the Hoe" to "Howl," though it may be one difficult for an Easterner to see.

Early San Francisco fiction was tough-minded, political, and naturalistic. No wonder the city later inspired Dashiell Hammett. Its fiction viewed the world mostly from the bottom up and vividly registered new social trends—from the labor movement and feminism to sexual freedom and environmental-ism—before they became mainstream. Artistic and social concerns mixed easily. The Bay Area not only liberated Charlotte Perkins Gilman to write "The Yellow Wallpaper," but also allowed her to organize the California Woman's Congress. The radical populism of London and Norris found enduring expression in later northern California writers like John Steinbeck, William Saroyan, Tillie Olsen, Oscar Lewis, Wallace Stegner, Janet Lewis, Amy Tan, and Maxine Hong Kingston just as it attracted and influenced a special sort of literary immigrant like Henry Miller, Kay Boyle, and Walter Van Tilburg Clark. Even its visionaries like Philip K. Dick and Richard Brautigan were anti-authoritarian and democratic. California is surely the only state that nearly elected a Naturalist novelist governor—muckraker Upton Sinclair narrowly missed winning in 1934. Who can blame an aesthete like Gertrude Stein for escaping this gritty, populist, and fervently political milieu for the *l'art pour l'art* freedom of Paris?

Populist modernism and Naturalist fiction were two of the major ways in which San Francisco once helped shape American letters. For nearly a century, the city represented the unexplored and invigorating possibilities of a new democratic culture. It was, to borrow a phrase from poet-critic Jack Foley, the "powerful western star" of American literature.

II.

"O powerful western fallen star"
    —Walt Whitman, "When Lilacs Last in
    the Dooryard Bloom'd" (1865)

Today California is—by a huge margin—the richest and most populous state in the union (with over 30 million people compared to New York's 18 million). The San Francisco metropolitan area in particular has grown immensely with nearly 7 million people living between Silicon Valley and the Golden Gate. If real estate prices are a reliable measure, the Bay Area is the most desirable place to live in the continental United States. The population is notably affluent and well educated. San

Francisco itself is often considered the most beautiful big city in North America. It is also a renowned center of music and the visual arts. What a smart, sophisticated, and pleasant place to live.

And yet San Francisco no longer ranks as an influential literary center. The demise of its cultural power does not result from a paucity of talent. The Bay Area probably has more established literary writers currently than any other urban area except New York and Boston. Within a twenty-mile radius of the Golden Gate Bridge one can find such diversely distinguished figures as Czeslaw Milosz, Thom Gunn, Carolyn Kizer, Amy Tan, Maxine Hong Kingston, Robert Hass, Mary Gaitskill, Tillie Olsen, Robert Silverberg, Kay Ryan, Anne Lamott, Gary Snyder, Al Young, Jack Foley, Edgar Bowers, Armisted Maupin, Ishmael Reed, Ron Hansen, Isabelle Allende, Lawrence Ferlinghetti, and Richard Rodriguez. The Bay Area is also ringed by major universities—Berkeley, Stanford, San Francisco State, the University of San Francisco, San Jose State, and others—that employ thousands of academics, including hundreds of critics and writers.

What San Francisco—and by extension all West Coast cities—lacks is a vital and complete literary milieu. In 1899 an aspiring author could come to the city and make a living writing while mastering the craft. There was a diverse literary ecosystem of newspapers, magazines, publishers, and theaters that not only fostered but also promoted local talent. Today the publishers have mostly moved to New York. The newspapers have either folded up or downsized by using wire service copy to fill their pages. The theaters perform plays from New York and London. Few national magazines still publish in San Francisco. There are numerous literary journals in Northern California most with limited circulation, but only *Threepenny Review* commands national readership. Most major literary magazines quickly fail like Francis Ford Coppola's *City*, Evan Connell and William Ryan's *Contact*, Al Young and Ishmael Reed's *Yardbird Reader*, and George Hitchcock's *San Francisco Review*—to name only four particularly ambitious and short-lived examples. In California, literary magazines almost inevitably become events—sometimes important ones—rather than ongoing enterprises.

Ironically, however, even success proves fatal to local culture. *Rolling Stone*, the quintessential San Francisco magazine, grew so large that it eventually moved to New York. Why did the booming journal leave its adoring hometown? Because New York—so insiders later admitted—was where the best freelance writers and advertising revenues were. The economics of contemporary publishing favor large journals located in the Northeast. After the failure of *City*, Coppola began his next literary magazine, *Zoetrope: All Story*, in Manhattan, although he continues to live in the Bay Area. The few large magazines remaining in San Francisco, like *Wired* and *Salon*, are nearly all related to computers and tied to the expertise and advertising base of Silicon Valley. There are no longer enough non-technical journals to create the critical mass necessary for a thriving world of freelance writers. To have a literary career, young Bay Area writers must enter the academy, survive on non-literary jobs, or, like *Rolling Stone*, move to New York.

The term *critical mass* may be a metaphor, but it is an illuminating one for understanding cultural life. In nuclear physics, critical mass refers to the minimum amount of fissionable material necessary to create a self-sustaining chain reaction. Something similar occurs in urban culture. A city or region needs a certain critical mass of enterprise and opportunity to create a self-sustaining local culture. Part of the reason is pure economics: artists need employment. Post-World War II Los Angeles had dozens of nightclubs and dance halls that provided jobs for jazz musicians, even rank beginners. There was also abundant work in film and television studios, as well as numerous local record labels. These various institutions provided the economic base for artistic vitality. The wealth of employment for jazz musicians in LA also created a fluid local culture in which soloists and sidemen could move from club to club and group to group without penalty. One quarrel did not end a career, or undistinguished colleagues permanently stifle a strong soloist. Musicians followed opportunities according to their temperament or instinct, and created a living tradition that focused and developed local talent. The result was the great West Coast jazz movement of the 1950s. Dozens of major players appeared seemingly *ex nihilo* from the streets of Los Angeles—Art Pepper, Chet Baker, Charles Mingus, Dexter Gordon, Hampton Hawes, Zoot Sims, and Eric Dolphy, to name only a few. No single intelligence or program willed this international phenomenon into being. It grew naturally out of a dynamic milieu that gave public context to individual talent—and it created art at once local but worthy of export.

If literature is an affair of individual genius, it is also the product of special circumstances in specific places. Fourteenth-century Florence, eighteenth-century London, nineteenth-century Paris created extraordinary literature because these milieus provided ample opportunity for diverse talents to develop and succeed. No poet can fail to note how often great writers appear in groups often surrounded by secondary (but still genuine) talents, as in 1920s Paris where Ernest Hemingway, F. Scott Fitzgerald, Ezra Pound, Gertrude Stein, Archibald MacLeish, E. E. Cummings, Malcolm Cowley, and other émigrés shaped modern American literature. Whether through competition or companionship, great talents spur each other on.

San Francisco once provided critical mass for a thriving literary culture. A writer fired from one paper could quickly find another post. A strong talent at one journal could be attracted to a better-paying position at another. There was room for literary feuds and rivalry—the necessary friction of cultural life. In true bohemian fashion, the various arts intermingled promiscuously. Poets Weldon Kees and James Broughton became filmmakers. Kees also wrote and produced the *Poets' Follies*, a literary cabaret whose cast encompassed writers, jazz musicians, actors, and printers, including Ferlinghetti, Adrian Wilson, and Phyllis Diller. William Everson developed into one of America's greatest fine-press printers—not a surprising turn of events in a city that had recently become the nation's leading center for the book arts. Bay Area printers published local writers in superbly designed letterpress editions. Adrian Wilson issued Kees's last book, *Poems: 1947-1954.* Jane Grabhorn's famed Colt Press printed Janet Lewis's *The Wife of Martin Guerre* (1941). Meanwhile Ferlinghetti opened the originally all-paperback City Lights Books and soon began publishing inexpensive pocket-sized editions of new poetry, including Allen Ginsberg's *Howl* (1956), which went on to sell more than eight hundred thousand copies. Rexroth helped found KPFA, the first listener-supported radio station where Kees and Pauline Kael hosted a talk show on film. The newsroom and bohemia together created a culture of local character and international stature.

III.

"There is only one trouble about the renaissance in San Francisco. It is too far away from
the literary market place."
    —Kenneth Rexroth, *The Alternative
    Society* (1970)

A Bay Area writer may still win a national reputation—witness the fame of Anne Lamott or Amy Tan—but that notoriety will be brokered, built, and administered elsewhere. San Francisco still produces literature, but it no longer exports much literary opinion. In American cultural life, opinion and reputation remain a mostly Northeastern monopoly. That is where one finds the vast majority of publishers, editors, agents, reviewers, arts administrators, foundation directors, prize committees, and literary institutes. The South understood this cultural imbalance early on, and it countered Yankee imperialism by developing a powerful alternative network of literary quarterlies like the *Southern Review*, *Sewanee Review*, *Georgia Review*, and *Virginia Quarterly Review*. These journals provide substantial critical coverage of regional writing and discuss national trends from a Southern perspective. As a result, the South has both maintained and evolved its regional character.

Significantly, there is not a single major literary quarterly currently published in California. Indeed, there has never been one that lasted beyond a few issues. *San Francisco Review* probably set a record in the early Sixties by publishing twelve issues. Moreover many—perhaps most—California journals like *ZYZZYVA* publish neither critical essays nor reviews. The best San Francisco now manages is the Sunday *Chronicle Book Review*, which publishes a few pages of extremely short and mostly positive notices—a *USA Today* approach to criticism. Under such conditions, even a good critic like Tom Clark hardly manages to say anything interesting. Only the two Berkeley-based tabloids, *Threepenny Review* and *Poetry Flash*, include a significant amount of literary criticism. (Pundits are never in short supply in Berkeley, which is probably why it produced—albeit twenty-five years ago—the last influential local literary trend, Language Poetry.) The other journals mostly leave opinion making to the East, and the results are tangible. There are single city blocks in Manhattan that generate more national literary opinion than all of Northern California.

The absence of quarterlies and other opinion-making journals will seem trivial only to those who do not understand how much the cultural milieu of a city nurtures or stifles local talent. Raw artistic talent is abundant. What is truly rare are the cultural circumstances, attitudes, and institutions to develop and perfect it. Few American cities have ever managed to foster a vibrant literary milieu of international significance—perhaps only Boston, New York, Chicago, and San Francisco. American literature has most often been an affair of isolated genius or small coterie.

San Francisco's current inability to create a critical milieu has a subtle but profound effect on local culture. First, it relegates the examination and evaluation of local art and literature to editors and critics three thousand miles away. But it also limits the options for serious young writers. The best critical minds either enter the university where they focus on the professional discourse of their academic discipline, or they publish in the East. Yvor Winters, the only major New Critic to live west of Ohio, published almost solely in Eastern journals like the *Hudson Review*, *New Republic*, and *Hound and Horn*. The closest he regularly got to California was *Poetry* in Chicago. More recently Winters's former student, Robert Hass, publishes his poetry column in the *Washington Post Book World*. Only after

Eastern validation did his column become reprinted locally. The same situation has existed for many California writers from Raymond Chandler to Joan Didion. They lived in the West but published in the East. They achieved local reputation only by gaining national recognition. The situation does not necessarily rob the local scene of talent, but it does make it harder for an idiosyncratic regional talent to be heard. And it considerably weakens the relationship between the writer and the local audience. They will no longer directly collaborate in creating a city or region's literary image of itself. That definition will probably be filtered though a New Yorker.

IV.

"Out here you can gravitate to places like San Francisco or Los Angeles where life is easy in terms of climate. You find yourself falling into pockets of your own kind where there is no necessity for struggle."
—William Everson, "The Archetype of the West" (1982)

No one has ever adequately explained why California has failed to develop influential institutions of literary opinion and reputation. If Gambier, Ohio and Baton Rouge, Louisiana can create important quarterlies, why can't San Francisco or Los Angeles? Why, too, is almost every major literary award —the Pulitzer, National Book Award, Bollingen, National Arts Medal, Frost Medal, Tanning, Caldecott, PEN/Faulkner, Leonore Marshall, and so on—administered somewhere along the Northeast Corridor? Wealth is surely not the issue—unless perversely California is too comfortably affluent to care much about literature. The newness of West Coast urban centers initially seems a plausible explanation for the cultural imbalance—until one notices that San Francisco currently exercises less influence than it did in 1899 or 1959.

New Yorkers, of course, believe they know the answer to California's cultural inferiority. The weather is too good; Californians simply don't suffer enough. This is the Woody Allen theory of West Coast culture, and it reveals far more about Northeastern fantasy life than it does about the nature of the West. If a temperate climate destroyed intellectual and artistic development, how does one explain Athens, Rome, Florence, and the rest of Mediterranean culture? And yet perhaps California's intellectual reticence does have something to do with the characteristic geography and history of the urban West.

Modern Western cities are built horizontally across huge stretches of land crossed by highways. The scale of Los Angeles, San Diego, San Jose, Las Vegas, and Seattle is not designed for the urban pedestrian. These cities are experienced most naturally from an automobile. The "neighborhoods" of Los Angeles are not square sections of the city, but the long horizontal axes of the major boulevards—Wilshire, Sunset, La Cienega—stretching across town. Even San Francisco, which was once a European-scale centralized city, has now developed into a vast and complex megalopolis linked by bridges and freeways across six counties. The automobile protectively seals the driver from both the city and other people. The communal exhilaration of the crowds and the chance encounters of the city pedestrian are alien to the automobile commuter who moves privately from home to workplace, and then back again. The Western commuter's life may not be lonely, but it is mostly solitary.

In the major Eastern literary centers—New York, Boston, and Washington—cultural life tends to be public and social. The sheer density of literary activities ensures that writers constantly meet one another—by design or chance. Accidental friendships result in new artistic ventures—magazines, theater companies, reading series, conferences, or collaborations. Rivals or enemies frequently cross paths—in editorial offices, prize committees, public panels, and at social functions. Private arguments become played out in public print. Take, for example, the countless volleys fired by New York intellectuals during the Culture Wars of the 1980s in journals like *Commentary*, *New Criterion, Nation, New Leader*, *Hudson Review*, and *New York Review of Books*. Merely the literary articles and essays could fill a sizeable bookshelf, and they created a national debate on the topic. Northeastern literary culture thrives on argument and invective. New York intellectuals like Alfred Kazin, Hilton Kramer, Susan Sontag, Norman Podhoretz, and Irving Howe did not become famous for keeping opinions to themselves. They strove to make them public policy. And they often succeeded.

Western literary life, by contrast, tends to be private and individualistic. Writers live far apart, and there are few occasions that bring them together in significant numbers. A California writer is more likely to see local colleagues in a Manhattan publisher's office than near home. Accidental meetings rarely occur, and hostile literati can easily avoid one another forever. In the process Western writers gain privacy but lose the considerable intellectual energy of social interaction, which is especially crucial both to criticism where ideas are rehearsed and even discovered in unplanned conversations and arguments and to institution-building, which necessarily depends on collaboration and community. Solitary and reflective, the Western writer is also often skeptical about the merits of the intrinsically social acts of criticism and institutional organization.

The Western writer's most influential relationship is usually not with the cultural milieu but the natural environment. Jeffers's lines from "Boats in a Fog" express an idea that is repeated in one way or another through a dozen major California writers:

> . . . all the arts lose virtue
> Against the essential reality
> Of creatures going about their business among the equally
> Earnest elements of nature.

When urban culture and the natural world compete in the imagination of a Western writer, nature always wins.

If New York literary life can be exemplified by figures like Lionel Trilling or Irving Howe—unadulterated urbanites—then California can be represented by writers like Wallace Stegner or Jeffers, true intellectuals but also naturalists and outdoorsmen. One can no more imagine Trilling in a pup tent than Jeffers at a Manhattan PEN conference. Rexroth hiked and camped for recreation. Frank O'Hara visited painters' studios for gossip and conversation. Both writers lived the values of the local culture.

The differences between New York and San Francisco were less marked fifty years ago. San Francisco still had an active and independent-minded bohemia full of influential writers, musicians, and artists. Rexroth, Kees, Ginsberg, Connell, Duncan, and others argued aesthetics and ideology in North Beach cafes while in local nightclubs, Paul Desmond, Dave Brubeck, Vince Guaraldi, or Cal Tjader were changing the course of modern jazz—actively recorded by Fantasy Records in Berkeley. Richard Diebenkorn, Elmer Bischoff, David Park, and Nathan Oliviera adventurously adapted the techniques of Abstract Expressionism to figurative painting. But as Bay Area intellectual life spread out and suburbanized, bohemia slowly broke up. Artists and writers took university jobs or moved to Sonoma or Santa Cruz, and the city gradually lost its cultural independence and vitality. Today San Francisco is no longer an active literary center, merely a geographical one for the dozens of important writers living in and around it. What Oakland-born Gertrude Stein said rather unfairly in 1937 about her hometown now seems prophetic of the sprawling and unfocused Bay Area: "There is no there there."

V.

"What is West Coast jazz? It's whatever the East Coast critics say it is."
　　—Unidentified West Coast jazz
　　musician (quoted in Ted Gioia's *West Coast Jazz* [1992])

The effects of California's remoteness from the centers of literary power are obvious. It is more difficult to create and sustain a major literary reputation from the West Coast. Not a single Californian—and only one West Coast resident—was appointed as Consultant in Poetry to the Library of Congress in its entire fifty-year history. Even after the position was elevated by Congress into the Poet Laureate, only one Californian, Robert

Hass, has served in the sixty-two years of the office. It took only fifty-one years for a California poet to receive the Pulitzer Prize—George Oppen in 1969—but the winner at least had the good manners to have been born in New York.

Neither Jeffers nor Winters, Rexroth nor Duncan, Miles nor Everson ever won a Pulitzer. Did these estimable West Coast writers lose to greater talents? An examination of the Pulitzer winners suggests that literary quality mattered less than proximity to the Manhattan-based committee. For example, in the two decades that Jeffers published his best collections—from *The Women at Point Sur* (1927) through *Hungerfield* (1945)—the prize went to New York writers, Leonora Speyer, Audrey Wurdermann, William Rose Benét, Robert P. T. Coffin, Marya Zaturenska, Mark Van Doren, and Leonard Bacon, a New York-born Rhode Islander. (The Maine-born Coffin taught in New York at the time of his award.) Is even the best of these poets remotely comparable to Jeffers? A region unable to articulate and advance its native arts will find them ignored in the cultural capitals. Such marginalization has another destructive long-term effect. Overwhelmed by the mainstream canon, regions gradually lose the memory of their own traditions and accomplishments.

Criticism and creativity also reinforce one another. The informed and demanding discussion fostered by quarterlies and other serious journals helps readers understand and evaluate new literary work. The sustained critical attention of Southern quarterlies frames the poetry and fiction published in the same pages. It informs, enlarges, and sustains an audience. Cursory newspaper coverage is no substitute for serious criticism, which provides not only a context for new work but also possible criteria to judge it. When a region loses—or never establishes—a local critical milieu, the culture is diminished both inwardly and outwardly. Inwardly, it lacks local pressure for artistic excellence and authenticity. Outwardly, it offers the broader world no clear articulation of local goals and values.

Lacking a vital critical milieu, well-intentioned regional literati usually practice boosterism—the uncritical praise of all things local. Boosterism is not merely a poor substitute for arts criticism; it is its opposite, a slow poison to native excellence. Cities create artistic excellence by setting up standards to recognize and acclaim it. San Francisco once reveled in its own high standards. "It is my intention," wrote Ambrose Bierce, "to purify journalism in this town by instructing such writers as it is worthwhile to instruct, and assassinating those that it is not." Those sentiments might still be expressed in New York or London, but they are inconceivable in California. Out here it isn't chic to take literature so seriously.

Confidence is a necessary component of genius. Bierce believed that one person could make a difference to local culture. And West Coast literary history repeatedly demonstrates how influential a single writer or editor can be. Ferlinghetti virtually created the Beat movement with tiny City Lights' innovative Pocket Poets Series. John Martin of Black Sparrow transformed the down-and-out LA writer Charles Bukowski into an international celebrity. He also revived the reputations of John Fante and William Everson by publishing them in handsome standard editions. Although City Lights and Black Sparrow now seem to have aged as artistic enterprises along with their founders, their past achievements exemplify how much the survival of West Coast literature depends upon individual conviction and informed local sponsorship. Such enlightened investment is unlikely to come solely from commercial presses headquartered on the other side of the continent.

Please don't misunderstand this argument. The Bay Area is still a sophisticated and literate region. San Francisco remains one of the few American cities that sustains a local literary identity. Berkeley maintains a modest bohemia in the shadow of its great university. San Francisco also has a rare and admirable sense of its own tradition and achievements. It has even renamed streets, though admittedly very small ones, after local writers like Hammett, Kerouac, Bierce, and Ferlinghetti. No American city publicly honors literature more than San Francisco. There are even commercial tours of literary sites.

The problem with San Francisco's admirable civic identity is that it is necessarily retrospective. Europeans, who for obvious reasons, understand this cultural dilemma better than

Americans, use the term *Museum City* to describe a place that preserves its past artistic achievements but lacks present vitality. Literary San Francisco remains fixated in its last moment of national literary glory—the Beat movement of the 1950s. It is considered impolite, however, to remark that those celebrated events occurred half a century ago. The presence of Kenneth Rexroth Place and Jack Kerouac Street hardly compensate for the absence of current literary vitality. It is surely not coincidental that San Francisco's major industry is now tourism. One is reminded of contemporary New Orleans—a city where jazz is everywhere honored but in which almost no new jazz is created.

VI.

"Every night at the end of America
We taste our wine, looking at the Pacific.
How sad it is, the end of America!"
     —Louis Simpson, "Lines Written Near
     San Francisco" (1963)

That is the public reality of San Francisco literary life—and by extension that of most major American cities outside the Northeast Corridor. A reader might argue the interpretation of a particular detail, but the general situation is inarguably clear. The pertinent question is whether the collapse of local literary culture and the disappearance of urban bohemia matters much to the individual West Coast writer? The answer, I think, is both not at all and very much.

Both literary history and common sense suggest that strong and dedicated major talents will prevail, if not always thrive, under almost any conditions. If great writing can be managed in the Siberian gulag or a tuberculosis ward, then it can surely be performed in Pacific Heights or Mill Valley. Yet literary history also demonstrates that a vital urban culture has a special power to focus literary talent. Urban literary culture is not a precondition of good fiction or poetry—though it certainly is for drama—but it does seem to help. And its absence is keenly felt in the atomized and individualistic communities of the American West.

The mythology of the Western writer usually dwells on the romantic individual alone with nature—Jeffers brooding by the Pacific, lusty Henry Miller in Big Sur, or London on horseback beside the smoking ruins of Wolf House. The myth of heroic individualism, however, may not be a particularly useful way to imagine the real possibilities of West Coast literature. Perhaps the metaphor of a winemaker serves the purposes better. A vintner spends a lifetime understanding exactly what grows best in a particular climate and location and then masters the art of preserving that essence for future enjoyment in other places. The best California wines are local but also coveted and appreciated internationally.

The purpose of this essay has not been to answer questions but to raise them—questions, that is, that are unlikely to be asked in New York or Boston. Comparing contemporary San Francisco literary life with the cultural scene fifty or a hundred years ago suggests certain uncomfortable issues not only about California literary life but about all American regional culture. The central question is whether regional literature can maintain a meaningful identity—something beyond local color and superficial accent—in the face of the global standardization of electronic media and the centralization of national literary opinion in New York. While this question has been framed here in terms of Northern California, it pertains equally to New Orleans, Atlanta, Chicago, or St. Paul. Another issue is how literary enterprises and institutions of national importance can be created and maintained outside the Northeast. Is urban culture still a viable reality for American cities outside the Northeast corridor? Or is some new social means of concentrating human talent needed? Is the delocalized and disembodied cyberspace of the Internet the American writer's only alternative to New York? These questions are especially pressing in the West where huge distances separate urban areas and the major cities often lack identifiable centers. Does the concept of Western literature still have meaning as a collective entity, or does it exist only as a remote abstraction in the work of isolated individual writers?

These are not abstract issues to California writers. Any serious literary artist in California, at least one writing in English, feels the competing claims of language and experience. However deeply immersed in the classics of English, the writer cannot help noting how this rich and various literary heritage stands at one remove from the physical reality of the West. Our seasons, climate, landscape, wildlife, and history are alien to the world views of both England and New England. The world looks and feels different in California from the way it does in either York or New York—not only the natural landscape but also the urban one. California also sounds different. Spanish, not French, colors our regional accent. The deepest European roots are Latin and Catholic, not Anglo-Saxon and Puritan. Asia and Latin America are omnipresent influences. There is no use listening for a nightingale among the scrub oaks and chaparral. Our challenge is not only to find the right words to describe our new and complex experience but also to discover the right images, myths, concepts, and characters. For us, this is an essential task, and one impossible to have done elsewhere. We must describe a reality that has never been fully captured in English. The earlier traditions of English only partially clarify what it is we might say. California literature is our conversation between the past and present out of which we articulate ourselves.

Local culture matters because human existence is local. Events happen in specific places to particular people. The climate and culture of a city, the landscape and language of a region, shape its inhabitants. The universal is most cogently found in the particular. To be local is not necessarily to be provincial. Regional literature is often initially dismissed in literary capitals, but a huge proportion of the imaginative writing that survives from the past century proudly bears its regional accent. James Joyce, Thomas Hardy, W. B. Yeats, Constantine Cavafy, Italo Svevo, William Faulkner, Chinua Achebe, Robert Frost, and Willa Cather are all regional writers of international stature. Vital local culture enables writers to understand and articulate more of their own experience. Strong regional journals and institutions allow readers to discuss and evaluate local work from their own perspectives. In an age of global standardization, regional voices also remind both writer and reader that no life is lived generically. If the purpose of literature is truly, as the ancients insisted, to instruct and delight, then what better to understand and enjoy than the *here* and the *now*?

Ten San Francisco Literary Classics

1. *The Sea-Wolf* (1904) by Jack London. Although American literati don't read this adventure, it remains a masterpiece of naturalist fiction.

2. *The Devil's Dictionary* (1906) by Ambrose Bierce. Forget the Summer of Love. Bierce is the real voice of San Francisco—mordant, worldly, skeptical, and witty.

3. *Cawdor* (1928) by Robinson Jeffers. Wildly violent, sexual, and visionary, but probably the best book-length American narrative poem of the century.

4. *The Wife of Martin Guerre* (1941) by Janet Lewis. A forgotten masterpiece, often plagiarized but never equaled.

5. *Mrs. Bridge* (1959) and *Mr. Bridge* (1969) by Evan Connell Jr. Connell had to live in North Beach to write these two penetrating studies of Midwestern respectability.

6. *Poems: 1947-1954* (1954) by Weldon Kees. Printed in an edition of only a few hundred copies, it is the dark classic of San Francisco poetry.

7. *Birth of a Poet: The Santa Cruz Meditations* (1982) by William Everson. The best book ever written on the West Coast literary imagination.

8. *The Man with the Night Sweats* (1992) by Thom Gunn. An unforgettable and harrowing vision of mortality by San Francisco's best living poet.

9. *Days of Obligation: An Argument with My Mexican Father* (1992) by Richard Rodriguez. The book that explained my Mexican mother and grandfather to me.

10. *Flamingo Watching* (1994) by Kay Ryan. A book of poems so ingeniously inventive that it reminds me of why I love poetry.

Dana Gioia

Bohemia Lost*

After a century of extraordinary cultural influence, San Francisco is no longer America's second literary capital. Although the Bay Area remains home to many important established writers—from Czeslaw Milosz to Amy Tan—the city does not support the kind of vital urban milieu where young writers meet and collaborate to create the future.

One hundred years ago, San Francisco was the rising western boomtown that changed American literature. The genteel Eastern capitals of Boston and New York had never seen anything like the gritty realism of novelist Frank Norris, the street-smart vigor of Jack London, America's first great working-class writer, or the sardonic humor of *Examiner* journalist Ambrose Bierce, author of *The Devil's Dictionary*. Innovative and irreverent, the voice of the new Gold Rush seaport was at once populist and yet oddly international—reflecting the city's unique geography, history, and demographics.

For most of the twentieth century, San Francisco continued to be the guiding western star of American letters, a democratic, progressive, and bohemian alternative to the eastern literary establishment. Art happened differently out here. The Beat Movement may have included New Yorkers, like Allen Ginsberg and Lawrence Ferlinghetti, but it could only have

---

*From *San Francisco Magazine* (January 2000)

developed so boldly in the freewheeling milieu of North Beach. From barstools and café benches, intense young writers created an art at once local and internationally significant. Caffè Trieste once contributed more to American literature than most major universities do. Now it mostly serves cappuccino to conventioneers.

These days, the future seems limited for aspiring writers—at least those who face the mundane necessity of making a living. The area's recent prosperity has had the ironic effect of dramatically increasing the cost of living just as the number of commercial newspapers, magazines, and publishers has declined. Bay Area affluence means higher rents, not greater opportunities. Meanwhile, the geographic expansion and suburbanization of the San Francisco region, which now stretches from Santa Cruz to Santa Rosa, has slowly eroded the once-thriving bohemias of North Beach and Berkeley. Rather than arguing art and politics in a smoky corner of Vesuvio's all night, most writers keep commuter's hours in a hundred Northern California towns where affordable solitude has replaced communal solidarity.

Many believe a new bohemia will rise from the Internet among the literary zines and homepages. But can delocalized and disembodied cyberspace resurrect the powerful specificity of regional culture? The Web seems more likely to foster a generic nationalism. American letters needs an alternative to the cultural monolith of Manhattan.

Reinventing itself for the new millennium represents literary San Francisco's greatest challenge—but how it will happen remains a mystery. Perhaps all that's required is for the right people to meet serendipitously in a SoMa gallery. Let's hope they don't get stuck in traffic.

Howard Junker

"THUS DO I REFUTE GIOIA"

January 2000
To the Editor of *The Ruminator Review*:

A lot of things suck in the Bay Area—the Warriors, the 49ers, the theater, the layout of the new Main Library, the collection of the Museum of Modern Art, bagels . . . but the literary scene does not.

Dana Gioia is so estranged, so painfully oblivious, that if he weren't also so pompous and inaccurate, it would be cruel to take him to task.

Begin with simple statements of fact: 5 of the 21 writers he says live within 20 miles of the Golden Gate Bridge do not.

Then feast your eyes on such klutzy, pontifical sentences as: "Local culture matters because human existence is local."

Continue with the scope of his argument: only a third of his report deals with current events; the rest is historical maundering.

His lead takes the long view: "In 1899, San Francisco was a major literary center." Oh nonsense. The epicenter of American letters in 1899 was Rye, England, where Henry James had a neighbor named Stephen Crane. None of the five "local talents" Gioia cites—Bret Harte, Jack London, Edwin Markham, Frank Norris, Lincoln Steffens—can still be read with pleasure!

As for Gioia's claim that Markham's forgotten poem,

"The Man with the Hoe," is "the quintessential Bay Area poem," I don't think so. If there's anything us locals loathe paying attention to, it's agri-business. In any form, even historico-poetical.

I'm sorry Gioia feels so isolated and so negative about everything, but that's always been his problem, ever since he was a General Foods marketing manager and the real poets wouldn't give him no respect. Then he shot his mouth off as self-appointed champion of retro-verse, a pathetic interlude in the wishful thinking of Postmodernism.

Now he lives in self-imposed exile, 60 miles from the madding crowds of North Beach. And he wails about "California's remoteness from the centers of literary power."

Oh revelation! If only we had known.

But the truth is: Power is not what it's about, and centers no longer hold us in thrall.

Nobody in the Bay Area, except Gioia, still yearns for the smokey, boozey, dicta-spouting huddles of the *Partisan Review* crowd. Today's scene is open to the public at readings at our incredible array of bookstores. And at the vigorous writing programs at Mills, St. Mary's, SF State, Stanford, and USF. And at SUNY-Buffalo's website.

Somebody please tell Gioia that literate youngsters these days pull down obscene salaries as web-content providers!

(Gioia's riff on fifties jazz is such a retro-gem I forgive its irrelevance.)

I also forgive him for not acknowledging that ZYZZYVA has survived for 15 years, flourishing as a vehicle that discovers new writers! And that I don't publish criticism, because I don't want to, because I want to concentrate on original work—the hell with writing about writing. And that ZYZZYVA "commands a national readership," or at least has subscribers in every self-respecting state and is available in superstores everywhere.

In closing, I would like to extend our local canon to include a few folks Gioia couldn't bring himself to mention, although they live within an hour-and-a-half's drive of City Lights.

First of all, let's claim our native son: Robert Frost.*

Then let's hail our senior citizens, Herbert Gold, Carl Rakosi; our Squaw Valley Community of Writers, Blair Fuller, Oakley Hall; our New York Schoolers, Bill Berkson, Barbara Guest; our still-boyish Michael McClure; our pop stars, Terry McMillan, William North Patterson, Martin Cruz Smith, Danielle Steel; our Tuscan hausfrau, Frances Mayes; our lyrical Latino, Francisco X. Alarcón; our Language-types Peter Gizzi, Lyn Hejinian, Nathaniel Mackey, Michael Palmer, Aaron Shurin, Leslie Scalapino; our answer to Helen Vendler, Marjorie Perloff; our queerish experimentalists, Dodie Bellamy, Robert Glück, Kevin Killian; our Southern belles, Dorothy Allison, Alice Walker; our goodlooking cyberscribe, Po Bronson; our doyennes, Judy Grahn, Diane Johnson, Adrienne Rich; our futurist, Poul Anderson; our nonfictionists Terry Castle, Carol Field, Adam Hochschild, Orville Schell, Kevin Starr, Shelby Steele, David Rains Wallace; our bad boys, Jess Mowry and William T. Vollmann; our newcomer, Michael Chabon . . .

Not to mention: Maxine Chernoff, Justin Chin, Victor Hernandez Cruz, Lynn Freed, Brenda Hillman, Jane Hirshfield, Ginu Kamani, Sandra McPherson, Clarence Major, Jack Marshall, Stephen Mitchell, Bharati Mukherjee, Ishmael Reed, Gary Soto, Tobias Wolff . . . Most of whom have appeared in ZYZZYVA.

Finally, our 26 billionaires. And our superstars: Danny Glover, Carlos Santana, Sharon Stone, Robin Williams, Alice Waters. . . .

---

*Would that Robert Frost lived "within an hour-and-a-half's drive of City Lights"!—Ed.

Jonah Raskin

LOCAL LITERARY SCENE
IS WORTH CELEBRATING

My friend Dana Gioia—who lives on a hilltop in Sonoma County and who churns out distinctly good poetry and trenchant literary criticism—has an odd take these days on the San Francisco Bay Area as a literary region. In the winter 1999-2000 issue of *The Hungry Mind Review*, Gioia complains that our part of the country has gone down hill since the glory days of the late 19th century when Mark Twain and Frank Norris held sway here.

I suppose he has a point. It's hard to go up hill, culturally speaking, from Mark Twain. Then again, the idea of measuring cultures and authors in terms of rising and falling like the barometer or the stock market doesn't sit well with me.

Creative writers are always among us, expressing themselves and giving voice to the voiceless. Those who sit around lamenting a glorious cultural past seem to me to be embarking on a lost cause.

When I look at the literary scene here in Sonoma County and in the San Francisco Bay Area as a whole, what strikes me is not the decline of the culture but its richness and diversity. Sure, we don't have a Mark Twain, but we do have some mighty fine writers with international reputations, as Gioia himself admits: Greg Sarris, Maxine Hong Kingston, Amy Tan, Alice Walker, Robert Hass and Carolyn Kizer to name just a few. There are many talented and productive Northern

California authors, including Gerald Haslam, Don Emblem, Michelle Anna Jordan, Bill Barich, Robin Beeman, Clarice Stazz, and David Bromige.

Gioia complains there is "no vital and complete literary milieu." But almost everywhere I turn I find a poetry reading, a book club discussion, an author signing, a writing group.

Gioia complains that there are no landmark literary journals here and that "San Francisco no longer exports much literary opinion." Granted, there's nothing like *Les Temps Modernes*, the intellectually towering magazine that Jean-Paul Sartre and Simone de Beauvoir edited, and there's no *Overland Monthly*, either, the pioneering San Francisco magazine that was initially edited by Bret Harte. But there's lots of solid reviewing at newspapers from San Jose to Sacramento, and there are lots of authors—like Wendy Lesser, Ishmael Reed and Tom Clark—who write with passion and clarity about our culture for an international audience. Gioia himself is one of Sonoma County's biggest and best literary exports.

Regionalism isn't dead and buried, not by a long shot. It has, however, been made over, and sometimes it's not easily recognizable. It's not the old regionalism in part because our region has been profoundly transformed in the past 100 years. Today's regionalism has roots here and branches that spread across the globe. It's a regionalism that belongs to no one ethnic group, literary elite or generation, and it's in the process of being redefined all the time by the successive waves of new immigrants who arrive here from El Salvador, Laos, Vietnam, China, India and beyond. It's a regionalism that refuses to obey rules or to stay within boundaries.

If you want to see for yourself, might I suggest that you look at books that were published last year by Northern California writers. Here are a few: Alfredo Vea's novel *Gods Go Begging*, Bill Barich's collection of essays *This Sporting Life*, Armando Garcia-Davilla's bilingual poetry *Out of My Heart*, Denny Bozman-Moss's illustrated children's story *Gordon, The Magic Turtle* and J.S. Holliday's historical study *Rush for Riches*.

Unlike Dana Gioia, I'm not of a mind to lament, but

rather of a spirit to celebrate. What we have here, culturally speaking, seems awfully good indeed. Whether it's better or worse than the culture of the past is difficult if not impossible to measure, and perhaps it's beside the point. If you don't like what's published today, might I suggest that you sit down and write a book of your own. That's what it's all about: the dedicated writer at his or her desk, putting words down on paper or up on the screen.

Richard Silberg

ON "FALLEN WESTERN STAR"

Dana Gioia Stirs It Up
in the *Hungry Mind Review*

After twenty years in New York, most of them building a career as a businessman to support an impressive second career as a poet, translator, and critic, Dana Gioia returned with his family to California, his native state, to live in 1996. His opening salvo to the Bay Area literary community is "Fallen Western Star: The Decline of San Francisco as a Literary Region" in the Winter 1999-2000 issue of *Hungry Mind Review* [just renamed *Ruminator Review*] in which he argues that the Bay Area has become a literary has-been because it lacks a "complete literary milieu," which he defines as a "diverse literary ecosystem of newspapers, magazines, publishers, and theaters," and, most especially, major literary journals in whose pages critics might perform the weighty work of evaluating and defining our writing for us and the rest of the nation. Without that ecosystem and those critics, he feels, our writers—and he grants us copious talent—can only wander in a feckless solitude, within the echo chambers of individual genius, and without any defining influence over our own works or the literary opinion of America.

Now, until I read his essay, I had been thinking of the Bay Area as a hot spot for poetry in the country, equaled only by New York. It played a key role in the poetic revolution of the mid-twentieth century and in the development of Language poetry in the seventies and eighties. It teems with poets, a startling number of whom have names that are both "major" and "national"—two words that Gioia stresses—and it swarms with readings, residencies, workshops, festivals, and conferences. Furthermore, the Bay Area seems to be a magnet for poets from the rest of the nation. For instance, in the week that I write this, Robert Pinsky is coming back to his old stamping grounds to appear "in conversation" with Thom Gunn; Yusef Komunyakaa read last month at UC Berkeley, where he had been Holloway Lecturer some five or eight years ago; Anne Carson, the spectacular Canadian writer, is here and doing months of readings; Sharon Olds and Galway Kinnell stream across country from NYU each summer to do their week-long poetry workshop at Squaw Valley. So what gives? Why the extreme parallax between Gioia's and my own points of view?

Gioia is a critic with clout, one that I respect. He has a compact, cogent prose style, formidable literary erudition, and an obvious love for poetry. At the same time, though, he has a penchant for provocative half-truths, and in driving those home he sometimes misses what's right before his eyes. He demonstrated both when he made his mark as a critic in *Can Poetry Matter?* (reviewed in *Poetry Flash*, January 1993, Number 238), whose title essay was published in the *Atlantic Monthly*. There he took a one-sidedly negative view of the poetry "subculture" that's resulted from the explosion of Creative Writing programs in American colleges and universities, while completely missing off-campus developments like slams, open readings, and festivals, flowerings off the Beat re-invention of the poetry reading that branched up into spoken word in the nineties and has changed the American image of poetry as we enter a new century.

"Fallen Western Star," I think, is making similar mistakes. For starters, there seems to be a systematic logical problem with his argument. On the one hand, he tells us that, "Significantly, there is not a single major literary quarterly currently published in California. Indeed, there has never been one that lasted beyond a few issues." But, on the other hand, he's celebrating the Bay Area's literary past, Jeffers and Everson, Ginsberg, Josephine Miles and Robert Duncan—his essay details our current community's fall from their influence and splendor—but, if critics and major journals are so crucial, how did that splendid past ever get splendid?

Gioia does some twisting and turning to answer that question. He opens in 1899 when "San Francisco was a major literary center—a city where influential trends emerged and young writers achieved national reputations . . . Jack London, Bret Harte, Edwin Markham, Lincoln Steffens, and Frank Norris." Why was that? "In the days before television and radio, national taste and opinion were not yet created exclusively in broadcast capitals like New York and Los Angeles . . . San Francisco, which was then the center of William Randolph Hearst's newspaper empire and home to dozens of other journals, helped set the agenda of American literature." Or, hopping to mid-century, "William Everson developed into one of America's greatest fine-press printers—not a surprising turn of events in a city that had recently become the nation's leading center for the book arts." I bet there are a lot of fine-press printers working in the Bay Area right now who'd be pretty unhappy to learn that they've disappeared into thin air.

Perhaps the real howler of these twists, though, is Gioia's rationalization for the Beat explosion in mid-fifties San Francisco: "Ferlinghetti virtually created the Beat movement with tiny City Lights' innovative Pocket Poets series." I've got the greatest respect for Lawrence Ferlinghetti, as publisher, as poet, as his city's recent laureate, but I'm guessing he'd probably agree that the truth is almost diametrically opposite. City Lights was an unfledged small press with no cadres of supporting critics. It was the power of the young Ginsberg and his poem "Howl" that virtually created City Lights, the power of the Beats, themselves, the young Kerouac—Ferlinghetti's own *A Coney Island of the Mind*, published by New Directions in 1958, was one of the bestselling poetry books of all time— McClure, Corso, Snyder, Whalen, and the rest, the confluence of their accessible, prophetic, demotic poetry with a social movement, the embryo of the counterculture within the button-down, "gray flannel" fifties, all spiced by pornography trials, that attracted the national media and began to turn the consciousness of America inside out.

Which brings me to my central point. The half truth in Gioia's new essay is generated by the "Literary Region" of the title, its one block linkage of fiction and poetry. I don't think the Bay Area has ever been a major center for fiction, certainly when compared with the Southern tradition, New England, above all, New York. There have been many, many strong fiction writers here in recent decades, and Gioia names some of them, Tillie Olsen, Maxine Hong Kingston, Ron Hansen; and some that he doesn't name strike me, the late Gina Berriault, Molly Giles, Leonard Michaels, for a few. But the Bay Area's special strength, certainly since the forties, Rexroth, Duncan, two poets that Gioia never mentions, Jack Spicer and Robin Blaser, and whirling constellations of others, has been poetry.

I'm not at all sure, finally, why that's so. But there are significant differences between fiction and poetry, their publishing requirements, how they 'live' and radiate their respective verbal lives, that go a long way towards explaining why the Bay Area is, in fact, a poetry powerhouse without Gioia's "major literary quarterlies," "the vast majority of publishers, editors, agents, reviewers, arts administrators, foundation directors, prize committees . . . literary institutes," and so forth.

Fiction costs a lot more to publish. There's a lot more money to be made in fiction. And equally important, fiction is primarily a print medium. I want to come back to that in a moment when we talk about readings, but, economically, what it means is that the market for a novel or a book of short stories is not usually regional; rather, the readership for fiction is a print market, extending as far in every direction as the books can be advertised and distributed. The combination of these factors overlays narrative literature with questions of business and media strategy.

It would be overstating the case to say that poetry doesn't cost money to publish, to advertise. Certainly publishers of "major" poets adopt "national" strategies in their marketing, publish hardcover books in an initial printing, look to get their authors reviewed prominently, get them on radio or, God help us, TV, send them on cross-country reading tours. But even the most celebrated poets aren't hoping for a major motion picture—and the real life of poetry, poetry as it hunts and feeds and breeds across America, is much more local, moves much more in the media underbrush. The vast majority of poets publish their work in small, ephemeral magazines, in chapbooks, in inexpensive paperbacks. We're talking about student poets, young poets, community poets, rings and rings of progressive, avant-garde, rebel poets clustered hither and yon or, perhaps, more and more, communicating electronically.

But fiction and poetry don't differ just economically. A crucial difference, as I hinted just above, is the role of readings. The voice of fiction is pitched "out"; for the most part, it's, precisely, narrative, dealing in characterization, exposition, action. Poetry, on the other hand, subsists in language itself. Consequently, it's the most bodily, vocal, gestural of the verbal arts. There are fiction readings, certainly, but their audiences don't really "learn" much from the reading that they wouldn't experience by reading the book at home. Fiction readings are more celebrity affairs aimed at signing and selling. But poetry lives in readings; its life is dual, even schizzy, divided between the page and the voice. We might go so far as saying that the "true" poem exists somewhere "behind" the page and the voice in a mystical triangulation between the two. So the poetry reading is an intensely spiritual affair; it "completes" the poem; it unites poet and audience, when it works, communing in the "word."

The importance of the poetry reading can't, I think, be overemphasized. It means that, while fiction writers get their major payoff only in publication, in print, poets can sustain themselves artistically, spiritually, in communities of poets and lovers of poetry through readings and inexpensive publications. It means that, while fiction is a national or geographically indefinite medium, solitary affair of writer in one place, reader anywhere else with an expensive book, poetry nourishes itself regionally, communally, much more face to face, voice to voice.

We're in position now to understand why the great American poetry revolution of the mid-twentieth century came out of "nowhere." It was genuinely national. It included not just the Beats, the most accessible, overtly spiritual, the most overtly rebellious of these poets, but the Black Mountain poets, the New

York School poets, and maverick poets from San Francisco, Boston, Los Angeles and traveling steadily points elsewhere and between. These poets were brought to national attention through the publication of Donald M. Allen's *The New American Poetry*, most famous and explosive of poetry anthologies, a book that made the names of most of the poets in it, made Allen's name too, then an obscure young editor from the Bay Area, and that, doubtless, was helped towards publication by the growing fame of the Beats. In his Preface—the book was published in 1960—Allen wrote, "These new younger poets have written a large body of work, but most of what has been published so far has appeared only in a few little magazines, as broadsheets, pamphlets, and limited editions, or circulated in manuscript; a larger amount of it has reached its growing audience through poetry readings."

Let's translate this into Gioia's terms. We're talking about what was arguably the most influential group of poets since the Moderns, Pound, Eliot, Williams, Stevens, et. al. I count two Pulitzers among these forty-odd poets, Ashbery and Snyder; Ginsberg, probably the world's most famous poet, Charles Olson, Robert Creeley, Michael McClure, the then LeRoi Jones, Denise Levertov, as well as about half of the poets Gioia cites in his essay as defining poets of the Bay Area's glorious past, William Everson, Robert Duncan, Gary Snyder (once again), and Lawrence Ferlinghetti. *The New American Poetry* was a literary earthquake. I remember Stan Rice—a poet who spent some fifteen of his formative years in the Bay Area at San Francisco State's Creative Writing Department before he moved with his wife Anne Rice to Louisiana and found Knopf as his publisher—telling me he thumbed his way through three editions, literally pored them to pieces. I remember me, myself, a long-haired undergraduate, being blown into a metaphysical daze by poems like "Kaddish," Olson's "The Kingfishers," so many more.

And what was the role of the major literary journals in this revolution, *Hudson Review*, *Sewanee Review*, *New York Review of Books*, whose titles "Fallen Western Star" sucks on like candy? Zip. Nada. These poets and poetries were all being written in direct or indirect reaction to the New Critics who then ruled the American academy and to the poets they sanctioned and interpreted. Nor, let me make clear, am I attacking New Critical ideas of what a poem can be. I'm not attacking the lionized poets of that time either; Robert Lowell, Elizabeth Bishop are wonderful poets, Berryman, Jarrell—even John Crowe Ransom has real virtues—or the great Adrienne Rich, who now lives in Santa Cruz and was last in San Francisco in March as a nominee for the Bay Area Book Reviewers Association Award in poetry. I'm going, instead, for the plain truth that poetry has a wild, deep life and can seize our national consciousness without the aid of big money, high prestige literary organs.

The development of Language poetry through the seventies and mid-eighties proves the same point and one more I'd like to make here. Language poets, like the Beats before them, centered in New York and in the Bay Area. Compared to the mid-century wave of outside poetries—I would call them "progressive," as opposed to the Language movement which was a genuine, and difficult, avant-garde—this new wave was relatively narrowly based, not so seismic, cool and intellectual; but poetically of the first importance. Wherever one stood, or stands, on Language poetry, it changed the whole dialogue, and it continues to ripple in what's being written today, in the Bay Area and around the country.

It too rose to prominence without the aid of, indeed flat against, the establishment literary culture. Today many of these poets, Charles Bernstein, Barrett Watten, Bob Perelman, Ron Silliman, have professorships (all of them now live in the East or Midwest); Lyn Hejinian has taught at New College of California and recently at the Iowa Writers Workshop. A steady stream of books on Language and related experimental poetries flows off academic presses. Way back when, though, the movement sustained itself through circles of readings, small press publications—and criticism. Language poetry is undoubtedly the most self-critical—in the sense of self-promotion and self-definition through the critical writing and talks of its member poets—of any movement in literary history.

I'm using an exception, then, virtually a poetic singularity, to prove this rule: poets, beginning when? Coleridge? Johnson? have frequently been the most penetrating and effective critics of their own and others' work. Think of Mr. Pound or Mr. Eliot. Think of Charles Olson. Black Sparrow Press has published volumes of Olson and Creeley's correspondence. Poets usually write criticism whereas fiction writers usually don't. In recent Bay Area history we could cite Robert Duncan, William Everson, Robert Pinsky, Kathleen Fraser, Robert Hass, Alan Williamson, Alicia Ostriker, who was first published out here and visits regularly, Thom Gunn, Jack Marshall, Carolyn Kizer, Jane Hirshfield, Tom Clark, Joshua Clover, Jack Foley, John Oliver Simon, Rusty Morrison, on and on—not even mentioning the Language poets, some of whom I've named above. Poets are a critical bunch. They love to meditate about language, to talk about each others' work. It's through this process—along with publications and readings—criticism both formal and informal, written and verbal, that poetry advances its bushy, populous life and that movements frequently build themselves even unto national attention.

Compare these living facts with Gioia: "Criticism and creativity also reinforce one another. The informed and demanding discussion fostered by quarterlies and other serious journals helps readers understand and evaluate new literary work." And: "Lacking a vital critical milieu, well-intentioned regional literati usually practice boosterism—the uncritical praise of all things local." I'm not against journals; the more attention paid to poetry the better—and let me take this opportunity to say that I think Gioia is rather dismissive of the journals that do exist out here—but those words smell a little arrogant, controlling; and they're the words of a man who's pretty out of touch with "San Francisco as a Literary Region."

I've been detailing my disagreements with Gioia to show why I think a strongly argued essay is, nonetheless, flat wrong, but there's one passage in his piece that makes me begin to hear weird music, in which he seems to have entered a veritable twilight zone. "Modern Western cities are built horizontally across huge stretches of land crossed by highways," a scale "not designed for the urban pedestrian," he tells us, naming LA, San Diego, San Jose. San Francisco, he goes on, "which was once a European-scale centralized city, has now developed into a vast and complex megalopolis linked by bridges and freeways across six counties." So—in contrast to "major Eastern literary centers" where "cultural life tends to be public and social"— "Western literary life . . . tends to be private and individualistic. Writers live far apart, and there are few occasions that bring them together in significant numbers. A California writer is more likely to see local colleagues in a Manhattan publisher's office than near home." Where the hell are we here, riding the plains in Larry McMurtry's *Lonesome Dove*?! Did not Mr. Gioia meet Jack Foley and me when he read at Cody's some years back? And did the three of us not gather and schmooze at the Bay Area Book Reviewers Association reception on the occasion of his younger brother's winning an award for his book on jazz? Did he and I not schmooze again on at least two occasions when he came to Cody's to hear other poets read? There's no more social, more hooked-up large poetry scene in the country than the Bay Area's, and I've read often enough in New York to know that that's so; although I have not, alas, recently visited my Manhattan publisher's office. I invite Dana Gioia to open up the *Flash* Calendar section and look at the pages and pages of readings, open readings, slams, workshops, festivals, open houses, etc. He could come to Books by the Bay this summer, put on by the Independent Booksellers Association. He could come to Watershed next fall. He might actually meet some Western writers.

Returning to the topic at hand, though, I think Gioia has a somewhat unreal and cut-to-his-own-taste idea of what Bay Area writing is and should be. His opening tableau—the trendy, influential San Francisco of 1899—segues to the poet Edwin Markham's "The Man with the Hoe," first published in the *San Francisco Examiner* and reprinted in countless other papers and magazines, translated into more than forty languages. He mentions Markham and his poem also in *Can Poetry Matter?* And I understand his point there, that poetry once had the kind of central media pizzazz—which it's since lost—to seize the imagination of the literate public and become, as he says in this new essay, "a literary call to arms for the labor movement." Well and good. But in "Fallen Western Star" he's using it quite differently. He quotes the opening and the ending:

> Bowed by the weight of centuries he leans
> Upon his hoe and gazes on the ground,
> The emptiness of ages in his face,
> And on his back the burden of the world.
> . . .
> How will the Future reckon with this man?
> How answer his brute question in that hour
> When whirlwinds of rebellion shake all shores?
> How will it be with kingdoms and with kings—
> With those who shaped him to the thing he is—
> When this dumb terror shall rise to judge the world,
> After the silence of the centuries?

And then he maintains, "Although no one ever cites it as such, Markham's 'The Man with the Hoe' was and remains the quintessential Bay Area poem."

Well, I'm sorry, folks, but there are two reasons why it's never cited that way, and the first is that it's second-rate. "Bowed by the weight of centuries"? "The emptiness of ages"? ". . . the burden of the world"? Aren't those clichés? I'm not putting the poem down for what it was, for the sincerity of its feelings, or what it meant for a political cause. But Gioia's the man who's touting "criticism . . . informed and demanding discussion." "The Man with the Hoe" is wonderfully suited for political sloganeering because it's well meant, exciting, simplistic, and somewhat sentimental. Which puts its worth as a poem on a par with *Gone with the Wind* as a novel.

Diversity is one key to the vibrance of the Bay Area. It's obstreperous, experimental, so many poets hitting on so many other poets, trading or butting ideas. With the partial exception of New York School, every kind of poetry is happening out here, mainline, academic, Language, postmodern, New Formalist, rap, slam. Gioia, however, seems to have a definite program for Bay Area poetry. He wants to build it on "The Man with a Hoe." "It dramatizes the lone individual against the system . . .

the style is both visionary and naturalistic . . . The concerns are moral and political. . . . Finally, the poem is conceived for oral delivery—it is accessible, dramatic and auditory." For Gioia, "mutatis mutandis," the best of what's followed out here—he names Jeffers, Rexroth, Yvor Winters, Ginsberg, Duncan, Everson, Snyder, Miles, Ferlinghetti, and Gunn—shares in these qualities, partakes in "an essential line of development" from our man Markham. " . . . these poets share crucial assumptions that might best be called populist modernism . . . Poetry was not conceived as a self-enclosed text for private meditation but as a direct address to an audience." "Who can blame," he asks, "an aesthete like Gertrude Stein for escaping this gritty, populist, and fervently political milieu for the *l'art pour l'art* freedom of Paris?"

> This ocean, humiliating in its disguises
> Tougher than anything.
> No one listens to poetry. The ocean
> Does not mean to be listened to. A drop
> Or crash of water. It means
> Nothing.
> It
> Is bread and butter
> Pepper and salt. The death
> That young men hope for. Aimlessly
> It pounds the shore. White and aimless signals. No
> One listens to poetry.
>
> (first poem in *Language*, by Jack Spicer, 1964)

That's an often-quoted poem by Jack Spicer, an aesthete in Gioia's book, I'd guess—although I'd say he's closer to an "anti-aesthete aesthete"—someone, at any rate, never mentioned in "Fallen Western Star." Spicer, of course, is a crucial poet out here, with Duncan and Blaser, a triumvir of the "Berkeley Renaissance." So here we have the second reason— as if we really needed any—for the noncitation of Markham's poem: this whole program of Gioia's is procrustean. He's not the first to talk about Bay Area poetry as "populist modernist," to use his term as shorthand for the constellation of qualities he lists above. The idea is enlightening; in this case I'd say it's more than halfway true. But it's a long way from the whole story, and when it's claimed as such it becomes dogmatic, tedious. I'd be very surprised if Duncan or Ginsberg, were they with us, would accept Markham as their poetic grandad, but I'm quite sure the Language poets wouldn't, or scores of other innovative poets heating up the mix here.

So I'd advise Dana Gioia to settle in, open up his eyes and ears, because he really doesn't get it. In the sidebar to his essay, "Ten San Francisco Classics," he lists two living Bay Area poets, Thom Gunn and Kay Ryan. To be fair, the format is impossible. Ten out of past and present authors, not just poets but novelists and essayists. Still, what bothers me about his choices is that he's a New Formalist himself, and these two poets, Gunn and Ryan, both do a lot of their work in closed forms. They're both, I think, wonderful poets, no problem there. Gunn was a star in England when he came here in 1954, and he's certainly become one of our essential writers, a world writer, really, rather than just Bay Area or California. And Ryan deserves what Gioia says about her *Flamingo Watching*, "A book of poems so ingeniously inventive that it reminds me of why I love poetry." My problems are two, though: first, the programmatic feeling in his choices, New Formalist choosing two formal poets; and second, there are so many other poets out here equally deserving, poets who are stars around the country. How about Robert Hass, our Laureate from the 'hood, generally recognized as one of the key poets of these last several decades in America? How about the radiant Brenda Hillman with her sweet blending of lyric and postmodernism? How about June Jordan or Diane di Prima? Barbara Guest? What about Michael McClure, or Michael Palmer? Al Young? Juan Felipe Herrera? How about brilliant poets less known than they should be like David Meltzer or Jack Hirschman? Let's not forget Jane Hirshfield, Kathleen Fraser, August Kleinzahler. What about Gary Soto, or Philip Whalen? Joanne Kyger? Leslie Scalapino? What about Tom Clark, Ishmael Reed, or . . . but I think you get my drift.

David Mason

LETTER TO *POETRY FLASH*

24 May 2000
To the Editors of *Poetry Flash*:

I read (in your May/June 2000 issue) Richard Silberg's long blast against Dana Gioia's criticism with increasing dismay. As a Westerner (writing from Colorado), I found Gioia's analysis in "Fallen Western Star" calmly objective and helpful. As he did in his earlier essay, "Can Poetry Matter?," Gioia took a sociological view of an aspect of literary life and illuminated it in useful ways. The earlier essay offered criticisms of Creative Writing programs; rather than acknowledging the truth in these criticisms (I say this as a creative writing teacher), many readers reacted in print as if they had been personally attacked. The same has happened in a few responses to "Fallen Western Star." Howard Junker wrote an incoherent denunciation of Gioia that was published in *The Ruminator*, and now Mr. Silberg has written his own misguided response.

The problem is that he doesn't approach what Gioia actually wrote in his essay, but raises some of Gioia's questions only to respond with obliquely-related data and his own prejudicial statements. Gioia criticizes the lack of West Coast journals that print criticism as well as poetry and fiction, and Silberg responds by saying that criticism isn't really needed because poetry lives in performance. This is not an argument, and it

ignores the fact that virtually all of the poets he extols have ben-
efited not only from criticism printed in journals outside the
Bay Area, but also from publishers outside the state. Silberg's
essay is full of contradictory claims; he has difficulty sustaining
his argument in one area without defeating it in another. He ac-
cuses Gioia of being programmatic in choosing two poets,
Thom Gunn and Kay Ryan, as exemplars—this is supposed to
arise from Gioia's New Formalist bias because Gunn occasion-
ally writes in rhyme and meter, and Ryan uses rhyme. But Mr.
Silberg seems utterly programmatic in his opposition to what he
calls New Formalism, though he continually claims that he has
nothing personal against anyone. *He* has nothing against Gunn
and Ryan, but when *Gioia* praises them it must be tainted.

As a Westerner I find Gioia's description of western cities
and the influence of sprawl on cultural life utterly convincing.
Silberg responds that it can't be valid because he has schmoozed
with Gioia at lots of literary events. Again, he's not really re-
sponding to a thoughtful argument, just dismissing it out of
hand. I think we in the West had better ask ourselves why so
much of our cultural energy is spent in or sustained by the East.
I also believe Gioia was right years ago to make us think critically about Creative Writing programs; whatever their benefits
to our lives, they've done nothing whatsoever, as far as I can
see, to improve the quality of American literature. In short,
Gioia's sociological critiques, well researched and cogently argued, are helpful challenges to us. They should inspire serious
discussion, not defensiveness.

Jack Foley

THE BLACK HOLE OF CRITICISM

Richard Silberg on
Dana Gioia's "Fallen Western Star"

Richard Silberg and I are friends who often disagree on aesthetic matters. Usually we let it go at that—different strokes for different folks. We respect and admire each other's work, and that's usually enough. I think Richard Silberg is a brilliant poet and critic, and I enjoy reading his work whether I agree with it or not. In this case, however, I felt impelled to write back.

Dana Gioia has referred to himself as a "contrarian." His "Fallen Western Star" (*Ruminator Review*, formerly *Hungry Mind Review*, Winter 1999-2000) seems to me an enormously challenging article with historical implications of considerable interest. Thank the lord that somebody has finally *said* something about this problem. Gioia's piece is a breath of fresh air.

Like the earlier responses of Jonah Raskin ("Local Literary Scene Is Worth Celebrating," *The Press Democrat*, 12/15/99) and ZYZZYVA's Howard Junker, whose letter to *Ruminator Review* is both hilarious and substanceless ("I don't publish criticism, because I don't want to"), Richard Silberg's article misses both the point and the challenge of "Fallen Western Star": what he sees is a dark star, even—to make the metaphor a little more accurate—a black hole.

There's a personal element here as well. "Fallen Western Star" begins with a reference to my book O *Powerful Western Star* and to the line in Whitman's "When Lilacs Last in the Dooryard Bloom'd" which gave me my title. Dana's introduction to *O Powerful Western Star*—written despite the fact of our being in very different aesthethic camps—is generous to me personally and begins to raise some of the issues which show up in "Fallen Western Star":

> Although the Bay Area has played an important role in American letters since the days of Jack London, Frank Norris, and Ambrose Bierce, the region remains ignored or underrepresented in standard literary criticism and history. California poets in particular have suffered critical neglect. Poets as different as Robinson Jeffers, Yvor Winters, Kenneth Rexroth, William Everson, Josephine Miles, Edgar Bowers, and Weldon Kees all remain obscure or undervalued in the broader literary world. Only the Beats managed to capture and sustain national attention—mostly for socio-political reasons—and in the intervening half century California has slowly slipped in the national literary consciousness.
>
> The relative obscurity of California writers originates at least partly in local cultural conditions. The Bay Area has often celebrated its own literary talent, but it has seldom done much to preserve, study, and meaningfully debate local achievements. The apparatus of literary fame hardly exists locally. There are no great quarterlies in California, and few literary journals of any sort that publish essays and reviews. This lack of public critical discourse and serious reviewing has made it difficult to develop local critical talent anywhere outside the university. If California has never lacked major writers in the modern era, it has consistently lacked significant critics seriously engaged with local writers.

Richard's opening sentence, "After twenty years in New York, most of them building a career as a businessman to support an impressive second career as a poet, translator, and critic, Dana Gioia returned with his family to California, his native state, to live in 1996," suggests that Dana has been out of touch with California. Later, Silberg writes, "I'd advise Dana Gioia to settle in, open up his eyes and ears, because he really doesn't get it." Doesn't he, though.

During his stay on the east coast, Gioia made *many* trips to California, where he has family. Indeed, *all* his family lives in California. In addition, he is not exactly a newcomer: he has been here for *nearly five years*. (He arrived in *January* 1996.) Isn't that enough time to get a sense of what's going on? Certainly Boise State University's Western Writers Series (which includes monographs on people such as John Muir, Bret Harte, Zane Grey, Robinson Jeffers, Gary Snyder and Simon Ortiz) regards Dana as a Western writer: April Lindner, the author of the monograph on Dana, has much to say about him as a Westerner.

For Raskin, Junker and Silberg, the fact that Dana doesn't *agree* with them means that he must be missing something. If he weren't missing something, he would agree with them! That is an indication of their tolerance for genuine disagreement: he's just an outsider, don't listen to him, he's been in New York for twenty years. As it happens, Dana phoned me to read passages from "Fallen Western Star" as he was writing it—and to ask my opinion about certain points. He phoned others as well, such as Kevin Berger, the senior editor of *San Francisco Magazine* and a lifelong Bay Area resident. Whatever Silberg thinks about Dana's qualifications to be writing about the West, I don't believe he would describe Berger or me as outsiders. He knows very well that I have been in the midst of the poetry scene for the past fifteen years or so. And I agree with Dana's essay. Richard is defending something, but one can ask whether he is defending anything more than the status quo.

Richard attempts to discredit Dana by asserting that "he has a penchant for provocative half-truths, and in driving those home he sometimes misses what's right before his eyes." Again the implication is that if Dana understood the *whole* truth he would agree with Richard. Richard then goes on to a long and not very compelling discussion of the difference between fiction and poetry. "Fiction and poetry don't differ just economically," he writes,

> A crucial difference . . . is the role of readings. The voice of fiction is pitched "out"; for the most part, it's, precisely, narrative, dealing in characterization, exposition, action. Poetry, on the other hand, subsists in language itself. Consequently, it's the most bodily, vocal, gestural of the verbal arts. There are fiction readings, certainly, but their audiences don't really "learn" much

from the reading that they wouldn't experience by reading the book at home. Fiction readings are more celebrity affairs aimed at signing and selling. But poetry lives in its reading. . . .

There is much to object to in this confused passage. Does Richard really mean to imply that narrative, characterization, exposition and action exist in a novel apart from its language? Has he never read narrative poems like *The Iliad* or *Paradise Lost* or Yeats' *The Wandering of Oisin*—or some of the works currently being produced by New Formalists? What I find most obtuse in the passage, however, is Richard's bland assertion that "There are fiction readings, certainly, but their audiences don't really 'learn' much from the reading that they wouldn't experience by reading the book at home." I suggest that Richard listen to Jack Kerouac reading from *On the Road* on a recently released Rykodisc CD or hunt up the marvelous recording of James Joyce reading from *Finnegans Wake*. One can learn a great deal from those renditions, and the last I heard, both *On the Road* and *Finnegans Wake* were novels. Talk about half-truths!

Another example of half-truth in Richard's article is the moment when he complains about Dana's choice of Thom Gunn's *The Man with Night Sweats* and Kay Ryan's *Flamingo Watching* as among the "Ten San Francisco Literary Classics." Gioia, writes Silberg, is "a New Formalist himself, and these two poets, Gunn and Ryan, both do a lot of their work in closed forms." Well, Keats and Shelley did a lot of their work in closed forms, too. But, apart from that, Gunn's poetry is activated by a *tension* between closed and open forms, which exist in an uneasy relationship in his work—as they do in Gioia's. A lot of what Gunn writes is free verse. As for Ryan, she does not write in closed forms at all: Richard is simply wrong about this. This is Ryan's "Half a Loaf." It is one of the poems in *Flamingo Watching*, and its technique is no different from that of other poems in the book or from Ryan's work generally:

> The whole loaf's loft
> is halved in profile,
> like the standing side

of a bombed cathedral.

The cut face
of half a loaf
puckers a little.

The bread cells
are open and brittle
like touching coral.

It is nothing like the middle
of an uncut loaf,
nothing like a conceptual half
which stays moist.

I say do not adjust to half
unless you must.

There is some interesting and subtle rhyming in Ryan's poem. (My favorite is "moist" and "must.") Perhaps that's why Richard considered it to be a closed form. But it is not a closed form. It is free verse: it is not metrically consistent, and it is not trying to be. I would suggest that Richard consult Lewis Turco's *The Book of Forms* to find out what a closed form is. What is it he says about Dana? That "he sometimes misses what's right before his eyes"?

Like Raskin and Junker before him, Richard indulges in cheerleading for his team: "How about Robert Hass, our Laureate from the 'hood, generally recognized as one of the key poets of these last several decades in America? How about the radiant Brenda Hillman with her sweet blending of lyric and postmodernism? How about June Jordan or Diane di Prima? Barbara Guest?"

How about it, guys. Let's hear it for all of them. Gioia's essay *asserts* that there are many, many fine writers in the Bay Area. He is extremely explicit about this. His point, however, is that they don't *talk* to one another, that there is no means by which they can discuss issues of vital importance to their work. Does Richard believe that Barbara Guest phones up June Jordan to talk about her latest poem? *Poetry Flash* is virtually the *only* outlet for local criticism. "Western literary life . . . tends to be private and individualistic," writes Gioia. "Writers live far apart, and there are few occasions that bring them together in significant numbers." How does Richard handle this? The Bay Area, he says,

> swarms with readings, residencies, workshops, festivals, and conferences. Furthermore, the Bay Area seems to be a magnet for poets from the rest of the nation. For instance, in the week that I write this, Robert Pinsky is coming back to his old stamping grounds to appear "in conversation" with Thom Gunn; Yusef Komunyakaa read last month at UC Berkeley, where he had been Holloway Lecturer some five or eight years ago; Anne Carson, the spectacular Canadian writer, is here and doing months of readings; Sharon Olds and Galway Kinnell stream across country from NYU each summer to do their week-long poetry workshop at Squaw Valley.

The fact of writers "streaming across country" from New York to teach us how to write is hardly an example of the vitality of local culture. Nor are visiting professors or people on book tours who stop at the Bay Area among other places. More of Silberg's cheerleading. But you will notice that, here and elsewhere in the article, Richard doesn't name any of the intellectual issues that arise out of all this activity. If there is all this exchange going on—"readings, residencies, workshops, festivals, and conferences"—*what are the people attending them talking about?* What are the issues that define us as Westerners? Richard is silent on that because, evidently, he doesn't know. Surely out of all this mish-mash something must be coming, right? But is it?

Richard's ignorance of a genuine Western tradition is particularly striking in his remarks about Edwin Markham and about Gioia's discussion of Markham's poem, "The Man with the Hoe." "Well, I'm sorry, folks," Richard writes,

> but there are two reasons why [Markham's poem is never cited as the quintessential Bay Area poem], and the first is that it's second-rate. "Bowed by the weight of centuries"? "The emptiness of ages"? ". . . the burden of the world"? Aren't those clichés? I'm not putting the poem down for what it was, for the sincerity of its feelings, or what it meant for a political cause. But Gioia's

the man who's touting "criticism . . . informed and demanding discussion." "The Man with the Hoe" is wonderfully suited for political sloganeering. . . .

But Gioia is not the only person to find Markham, and particularly that poem, to be quintessentially Western. First published in 1976, William Everson's *Archetype West: The Pacific Coast as a Literary Region* is a brilliant examination of the coinciding of literature and region. "Markham," writes Everson, "is no longer highly regarded. He was, however, the first poet of the West to produce a poem that has entered world literature. Seventy years after its composition 'The Man with the Hoe' is still read and believed around the world." Everson even cites a connection—though not a direct, literary one—between "The Man with the Hoe" and Ginsberg's "Howl." Everson is writing of the forties:

> This accent on the spoken rather than the printed word, this devolution from the fixed standard of the page and its emphasis on dispassionate analysis which the eye implements, meant of course a rise in the *participation mystique* which [the Western] archetype favors, and which would later become one of the principal features of the Beat Generation. There were poetry readings earlier, of course, but attendance was usually confined to persons who knew beforehand the poet's representative works. Now the poetry reading was transformed from recital into *encounter*. This elimination of lecture hall distance between speaker and audience, this dependence on the primacy of voice, was crucial to the development of things in San Francisco. As we noted earlier it was Markham's direct reading that moved the editor of the San Francisco *Examiner* to instigate the breakthrough publication of "The Man with the Hoe." So it would be with *Howl*, which was "published" when it was first read in the old Six Gallery in the San Francisco Marina in the fall of 1955, and which gained a powerful reputation on platform well before it was issued in print.

Surely a poem to which Everson devotes so much of his book deserves better than Richard's curt dismissal of it as "wonderfully suited for political sloganeering." In his remarks about Markham, Dana Gioia attempts to recreate something of the consciousness with which the poem—which galvanized people worldwide—was received at the time of its initial appearance. He shows ways in which the poem might still interest contemporary readers. Richard treats "The Man with the Hoe" as if it were written last Friday; his dismissal of it is fairly well-written and somewhat amusing—as is the article generally—but it is also woefully ignorant and wildly unfair. Markham himself described the poem—accurately—as "a bit of verse that seems to have put into articulate form some of the questions troubling our consciousness at the end of the century" (*The Saturday Evening Post*, vol. 172, no. 25, 12/16/1899).

There are many other things to quarrel with in Richard's article. (I've said nothing about assertions like "the 'true' poem exists somewhere 'behind' the page and the voice in a mystical triangulation between the two.") But I want to conclude with a wonderful passage of Dana's about his experience of being a Western writer. Much of the passage appears in "Fallen Western Star," so Richard has read a good deal of it. He may even have read it when it first appeared in Heyday Books' *The Geography of Home*. What I am quoting here is the form in which I first encountered it. Despite its length, I immediately included it in *O Powerful Western Star*. It seemed to me something that needed to be said but had not been said. It seemed as well to arise out of a powerful understanding of what it means to live in the West. "I am Latin (Italian, Mexican, and American Indian)," writes Gioia,

> without a drop of British blood in my veins, but English is my tongue. It belongs to me as much as to any member of the House of Lords. The classics of English—Shakespeare, Milton, Pope, and Keats—are my classics. The myths and images of its literature are native to my imagination. And yet this rich literary past often stands at one remove from the experiential reality of the West. Our seasons, climate, landscape, natural life, and history are alien to the world-views of both England and New England. Spanish—not French—colors our regional accent. The world looks and feels different in California from the way it does in Massachusetts or Manchester—not only the natural landscape but also the urban one. There is no use listening for a nightingale

among the scrub oaks and chaparral. Our challenge is not only to find the right words to describe our experience but also to discover the right images, myths, and characters. We must describe a reality that has never been fully captured in English. Yet the earlier traditions of English help clarify what it is we might say. California poetry is our conversation between the past and present out of which we articulate ourselves.

I find that statement to be not only true but of an unmatched lyricism and eloquence. We ought to be trying to respond to the questions Dana Gioia's eloquent and enlightening essay gives rise to. Instead, we make fools of ourselves by pretending what he is telling us doesn't exist—and, like Richard Silberg, we see little but darkness.

*

Since "The Man with the Hoe" is no longer easily available to readers, I thought it would be useful to include it here. Let the reader decide about its value. Here are both the original and the revised versions:

The Man with the Hoe (Original Version)
Written after seeing Millet's World-Famous Painting

> God made man in His own image,
> in the image of God made He him.—*Genesis.*

Bowed by the weight of centuries he leans
Upon his hoe and gazes on the ground,
The emptiness of ages in his face,
And on his back the burden of the world.
Who made him dead to rapture and despair,
A thing that grieves not and that never hopes,
Stolid and stunned, a brother to the ox?
Who loosened and let down this brutal jaw?
Whose was the hand that slanted back this brow?
Whose breath blew out the light within this brain?

Is this the Thing the Lord God made and gave
To have dominion over sea and land;
To trace the stars and search the heavens for power;
To feel the passion of Eternity?

Is this the Dream He dreamed who shaped the suns
And pillared the blue firmament with light?
Down all the stretch of Hell to its last gulf
There is no shape more terrible than this—
More tongued with censure of the world's blind greed—
More filled with signs and portents for the soul—
More fraught with menace to the universe.

What gulfs between him and the seraphim!
Slave of the wheel of labor, what to him
Are Plato and the swing of Pleiades?
What the long reaches of the peaks of song,
The rift of dawn, the reddening of the rose?
Through this dread shape the suffering ages look;
Time's tragedy is in that aching stoop;
Through this dread shape humanity betrayed,
Plundered, profaned and disinherited,
Cries protest to the Judges of the World,
A protest that is also prophecy.

O masters, lords and rulers in all lands,
Is this the handiwork you give to God,
This monstrous thing distorted and soul-quenched?
How will you ever straighten up this shape;
Touch it again with immortality;
Give back the upward looking and the light;
Rebuild in it the music and the dream;
Make right the immemorial infamies,
Perfidious wrongs, immedicable woes?

O masters, lords and rulers in all lands,
How will the Future reckon with this Man?
How answer his brute question in that hour
When whirlwinds of rebellion shake the world?
How will it be with kingdoms and with kings—
With those who shaped him to the thing he is—
When this dumb Terror shall reply to God,
After the silence of the centuries.

(1899)

The Man with the Hoe (Revised Version)
Written after seeing Millet's world-famous
painting of a brutalized toiler

> God made man in His own image,
> in the image of God made He him.—*Genesis.*

Bowed by the weight of centuries he leans
Upon his hoe and gazes on the ground,
The emptiness of ages in his face,
And on his back the burden of the world.
Who made him dead to rapture and despair,
A thing that grieves not and that never hopes,
Stolid and stunned, a brother to the ox?
Who loosened and let down this brutal jaw?
Whose was the hand that slanted back this brow?
Whose breath blew out the light within this brain?

Is this the Thing the Lord God made and gave
To have dominion over sea and land;
To trace the stars and search the heavens for power;
To feel the passion of Eternity?
Is this the dream He dreamed who shaped the suns
And markt their ways upon the ancient deep?
Down all the caverns of Hell to their last gulf
There is no shape more terrible than this—
More tongued with censure of the world's blind greed—
More filled with signs and portents for the soul—
More packt with danger to the universe.

What gulfs between him and the seraphim!
Slave of the wheel of labor, what to him
Are Plato and the swing of Pleiades?
What the long reaches of the peaks of song,
The rift of dawn, the reddening of the rose?
Thru this dread shape the suffering ages look;
Time's tragedy is in that aching stoop;
Thru this dread shape humanity betrayed,
Plundered, profaned and disinherited,
Cries protest to the Judges of the World,
A protest that is also prophecy.

O masters, lords and rulers in all lands,
Is this the handiwork you give to God,
This monstrous thing distorted and soul-quenched?
How will you ever straighten up this shape;
Touch it again with immortality;
Give back the upward looking and the light;
Rebuild in it the music and the dream;
Make right the immemorial infamies,
Perfidious wrongs, immedicable woes?

O masters, lords and rulers in all lands,
How will the future reckon with this Man?
How answer his brute question in that hour
When whirlwinds of rebellion shake all shores?
How will it be with kingdoms and with kings—
With those who shaped him to the thing he is—
When this dumb Terror shall rise to judge the world,
After the silence of the centuries?

—Edwin Markham

Richard Silberg

RESPONSE TO JACK FOLEY

Maybe we can make a little progress by separating the questions.

Is the Bay Area a vital, influential poetry scene? I think the answer to that question has got to be yes. I'd guess Jack Foley would agree, if he could unhook his response from his zeal to defend Dana Gioia. There's no center of influence today in American poetry, geographically, as the Northeast was, for instance, among Modernists at the beginning of the twentieth century, or critically, as in the reign of the New Criticism into mid-century. Today, influence is multi-centered; poets are highly mobile; different poetries are highly interactive. But if you could take an infra-red photograph from the first reaches of space, high above the fray, the two major hot spots in America—virtually beyond question—would be New York and the Bay Area.

"The presence of Kenneth Rexroth Place and Jack Kerouac Street hardly compensate for the absence of current literary vitality." "Today San Francisco is no longer an active literary center, merely a geographical one for the dozens of important writers living in and around it." Those two separate quotes from "Fallen Western Star" sum up Dana's answer, and that was the bone in my throat when I read his essay. His voice is an important one; there are literary stakes, particularly among young poets deciding where they want to put their fire. So I felt he had to be answered.

Now, is there a dearth of criticism in the Bay Area? Should we welcome new journals onto the set? The answer to that question clearly ought to be yes as well.

But, for me, with two provisos.

First of all, it's axiomatic to Dana that the health of a literary region rests upon the health of its literary milieu, with a special emphasis on major literary journals. His assessment of the Bay Area is virtually a deduction from that principle. So I took pains to refute it.

One would never guess from Jack's response that I'd made any substantive arguments—he seems to be tiptoeing around the central points—but, actually, I made several. For the sake of space, let's distill them to one: the last two revolutions in American poetry, its profound quakes and shakes at mid-century and the narrower but still crucially important advent of Language poetry in the seventies and eighties, rolled forth without input from, in fact, against the grain of the literary establishments of their respective days. We're talking about what are certainly among the most influential, most powerful poetries of the later twentieth century, Beat, Black Mountain, New York School, Language, and the magnificent mavericks swarming in and thereabouts. Q.E.D.: There's no calculation of major journals, editors, agents that adds up to the life of a poetry.

My second proviso is more wide-ranging, and so it has the advantage of opening out our discussion—because I'm acutely conscious that for many of our readers, in LA, for instance, or Seattle, or New Mexico, this fine tooth back and forth on the merits or demerits of Bay Area poetry is just a local dustup. I'm sensing that Dana and I have rather different ideas of the function of criticism, with Jack seeming to side with Dana—although, actually, while he's under the impression that he's arguing Dana's point of view, on at least one point I think he's wangling way out on his own. So I'd like, briefly, to ponder one more question: just what is it we're expecting criticism to do for us?

Dana says quite a few things about criticism in "Fallen

Western Star," but let me focus on two. "Cities create artistic excellence by setting up standards to recognize and acclaim it." And just before that, "Lacking a vital critical milieu, well-intentioned regional literati usually practice boosterism—the uncritical praise of all things local." Together, those two statements set up separate realms, criticism and poetry, with criticism demanding, refining, forming what seems to be an impulsive but ignorant—again, just above the last quote he speaks of "The informed and demanding discussion fostered by quarterlies and other serious journals"—poetry. It's an attitude that gives critics a lot of credit and poets rather little, criticism as trainer and poetry as dog, so to speak.

Jack's ideas about criticism feel more duplex—in great part, I think, because of his contortions as self-appointed defender of Dana. There's a certain echoing of Dana's formative criticism idea, particularly in the sentence with which he ends that section of his response: "Surely out of all this mish-mash something must be coming, right? But is it?" implying, it would seem, that the mere activities of poets, the "readings, residencies, workshops, festivals, and conferences" to which his word "mish-mash" refers could hardly be shapely, could hardly be defining themselves in any important way without the above "informed and demanding discussion"—and I feel an uncharacteristic disdain radiating in Jack's "mish-mash" word choice.

The main idea this section puts forth, though, I would say, is the following: "His [Dana's] point, however, is that they don't talk to one another . . . Does Richard believe that Barbara Guest phones up June Jordan to talk about her latest poem?" I'm much more friendly to that idea of criticism as a medium for poets' mutually informing discussion. The only problem is that it isn't Dana's—it's Jack's, either a previous good idea, or one born out of his strained argumentative necessities.

Dana does say in his essay that Western writers don't talk to each other, but he's not referring to "talk" through essays back and forth in "major literary journals," nor to a kind of indirect discourse in which perceptive critics argue or synthesize widely differing poetics so that poets can understand each others' positions better. Weirdly, Dana means actual talk, itself.

"Western literary life . . . tends to be private and individualistic . . . Writers live far apart, and there are few occasions that bring them together in significant numbers." Jack quotes Dana in his response, deadpan, although he knows perfectly well it ain't remotely so—he, himself, has starred in inimitable person at quite a few of those "readings . . . festivals . . . conferences." Thence Dana's inexplicable misperception of Bay Area poetry, solitary, forest and freeway, transmutes to a rich, strange Habermasian idea of criticism.

Perhaps disingenuous, too, for all its sparkle. Very likely none of us besides Guest and Jordan knows what they've actually said to each other about poetry. But, of course, Jack's speaking metonymically, taking them as representative of writers with widely separated poetics. And he suggests this idea that criticism can cross the gap, help them to poetic discussion. I think he knows, though, that poets are not that different from other people when it comes to differences, political, say, or religious: poets tend to break into groups according to poetics and to do most of their talking with their own. Just where, I wonder, does Jack think this kind of cross-poetic dialogue is taking place? In New York, with all its journals and literary infrastructure? Is there, for instance, a lively colloquy between the Nuyorican Poets Cafe and the Poetry Society of America? Is it happening on the pages of the *Hudson Review*, *Sewanee Review*, the *New York Review of Books*? No, it's not, and I'm guessing that he knows that. It is happening in some places, though. I think the *American Poetry Review* in recent years has tried to become more of a bridging journal. And it's happening, to a certain extent in *Poetry Flash*—as Jack, himself, says—and very much with his help as one of our contributing editors. *Poetry Flash*, without any undue horn tooting, is a journal right here in the Bay Area, but serving a much wider area, that tries to bring poetries together.

We could talk a lot more about interaction between poetic schools, about places like Naropa and New College of California, for instance, but I want to get back to Dana's actual criticism, which is, as I've said, formative, disciplinary, one summed up for me by a phrase that critics often use, a phrase that's always irritated me, the book "under review."

Let me suggest another possibility, really another pole of the critical sphere. Poetry is inherently shapely, and shape-making; further, in its developing, changing "nature"—a problematic, essentialist word, but I'm trying to be brief—it's sublimely wise. As I suggested in my response to Dana, poets are usually also critics, and if we stop to think about it, most of what we really know, core knowledge in the sense of pithy ideas about poetry, comes not from critics but from poets. Think of Coleridge, Arnold, of Pound and Eliot, Surrealist and Futurist manifestos and elaborations, Olson and Creeley, Language critics, so many others. Think of "organic form"; composing not according to the "metronome" but in the cadence of the "musical phrase"; "objective correlative"; "lower limit speech, upper limit music"; "open field composition"; obviously, this could go pages and pages.

On the other hand, when I think of criticism that's really meant something to me, it tends to work either "above" or "below" this core knowledge formulated by poets, and, of course, the poetry itself. Above, we have the work of critics like Kenneth Burke, say, Northrop Frye, even Harold Bloom or Paul de Man, although his deconstructionist ideas also deeply irritate me. These men are writing a meta-criticism, reflections on literature in planes that really parallel philosophy or religion. Below, there's a mode of criticism exemplified by Hugh Kenner in his great books on Pound, on Eliot and Beckett. Kenner's books don't stand in judgment over their subjects; instead, they breathe forth these writers' spirits; they are profound appreciations. Many of Jack's fine essays are criticism of this type.

So, what about criticism of books "above review"? What about criticism that learns from poetry, that approaches it in a loving openness? And I don't mean by that a ga-ga servility, critics with something mushy or worshipful to say about everything they read. I don't mean not having standards; I'm talking about the attitude that poetry knows more than the critic does, so that one's standards are in flux as poetry is in flux. That's not very different, really, from the way scientists approach their material: they don't prejudge their data; they're informed by it.

There's some unfairness in what I'm saying. I've learned a good deal from reading Dana, and I think he's often perceptive. To finish the sentence about "informed and demanding discussion" that I cut off above, he thinks it "helps readers understand and evaluate new literary work." I'm all for that. I want good poets and their publishers to find good readers. I want us all to boogie. But, as I've already said, I'm troubled by the section in "Fallen Western Star" where Dana tries to type Bay Area poetry on "The Man with the Hoe." I'm bugged by pronouncements like, "Poetry was not conceived as a self-enclosed text for private meditation but as a direct address to an audience." There are a lot of fine poets around here with a very different take on that. I feel somewhat pinched by the way Dana and Jack harp on "regional" writing and the West. I'm not at all sure that that concept carries much water anymore in these fast traveling, electronic times.

My second proviso, then: let's have new critical journals; let's have "major" journals, but let them be open to the heavenly buzz, to the boogie profusion. Let them appreciate poetry that they love, or meditate on it, rather than pronounce upon it or train it to be the good poetry dog they pre-desire.

Those, I think, are the central issues. The questions from Jack's response are still hanging, though, his various skirmishing points. But my feeling is that we've already devoted enough precious print space to this debate, maybe too much. Is "The Man with the Hoe" in fact a bit clichéd and sentimental, or not? Does poetry have a special relationship with public readings, a central relationship intrinsic to poetic practice, that fiction really doesn't, or not? Was Dana's choice of Thom Gunn and Kay Ryan as the two star poets of the Bay Area rather narrow and programmatic in its taste, or not? These essays are available, Dana's, mine, Jack's—to the extent that they're of interest, a good thing. Why not let interested readers make up their minds on it all for themselves?

Jacqueline Marcus

DANA GIOIA'S "FALLEN WESTERN STAR"

Even if you don't agree with Dana Gioia's premise, that San Francisco "lacks a vital and complete literary milieu," you'd still have to concede that "Fallen Western Star" is a brilliant, engaging essay. You may or may not agree with Gioia's conclusion that New York City is the literary center for book promotions, journals, free-lance writers and advertisement, nevertheless—"Fallen Western Star" is an impressive assessment of Northern California's literary history of poetry. The fact that Dana Gioia's essay became a controversial subject the minute it appeared in *The Hungry Mind Review* (renamed *Ruminator Review)*—is, in my opinion, a good thing. In order to stir things up, you have to be an exceptionally good writer. So once again, Dana Gioia has driven the literary community (at least in the Bay Area) crazy. In this sense, I see Gioia as our community "gadfly" that provokes thought—he targets writers where it stings the most: right at their egos.

On the other side of the argument, Richard Silberg, Associate Editor of *Poetry Flash*, was one of the first Bay Area writers to disagree with Gioia's criticism of the cultural landscape of San Francisco, which Gioia believes is on the decline. Silberg writes in *Poetry Flash*:

> Diversity is one key to the vibrancy of the Bay Area. It's obstreperous, experimental, so many poets hitting on so many other poets, trading or butting ideas. With the partial exception

of New York School, every kind of poetry is happening out here, mainline, academic, Language, postmodern, New Formalist, rap, slam. Gioia, however, seems to have a definite program for Bay Area poetry. . . .

In either case, Gioia's "Fallen Western Star" is an example of narrative writing at its best. I enjoyed the way Gioia described the history of San Francisco's writers and musicians from post World War II jazz musicians to Robinson Jeffers. And although Silberg didn't particularly care for Gioia's selections, such as Markham's "The Man with the Hoe," Gioia's description of how that poem became internationally famous is fascinating:

> Newspapers were the Internet of the nineteenth century—a decentralized information system—and "The Man with the Hoe" was reprinted from paper to paper first across the United States and then abroad. Translated into more than forty languages, it was eventually republished in 10,000 newspapers and magazines. In the early twentieth century there was no more famous American poem than Markham's. The poet became an international celebrity, and the poem served as a literary call to arms for the labor movement—all of which began with the *San Francisco Examiner*.

According to Gioia, in those days, 1899, San Francisco was, as Jack Foley put it, the "powerful western star" of American literature.

I happened to catch Michael Kinsley one morning, editor of Slate.com, on C-SPAN's *Washington Journal*, address the question of how an editor selects material for publication. To paraphrase Mr. Kinsley, he said that you don't want commentaries that leave nothing to the imagination. You want to publish work that is controversial—otherwise, people will think it's boring.

Gioia's opinions may anger a good number of writers and readers, but the last thing they could ever say about his work is that it leaves nothing to the imagination or that it is boring. Interestingly enough, Gioia suggests that Bay Area writers have gone soft in this respect—as if our culture were an extension of the mild weather, and the Starbucks scene of suburbanite social gatherings. The days of "literary feuds and rivalry," wrote Gioia, "the necessary friction of cultural life," have all but disappeared in northern California. I'm not sure if that's true, but in any event, I think Gioia raises an important question as to whether or not San Francisco can compete, as a literary region, with New York City.

Michael Lind

LETTER TO *POETRY FLASH*

June 1, 2000
To the Editors:

Richard Silberg, in his criticism of Dana Gioia's essay, "Fallen Western Star," unwittingly provides confirmation of the point that Gioia made in his earlier essay "Can Poetry Matter?"— namely, that what passes for American poetry at the beginning of the twenty-first century is a game played among academics. Describing one such game, Language poetry, Silberg writes: "It too rose to prominence without the aid of, indeed flat against, the establishment literary culture. Today, many of these poets . . . have professorships. . . ." What? Some poets have found jobs as creative-writing instructors? Whoever heard of such a thing? The fact is that ever since the Fugitive/Agrarians, the "movements" in American poetry have by and large been ephemeral fashions designed and promoted to boost the careers of tiny cliques of ambitious professors, who are then dislodged by the next generation of academics leading the next "movement."

Take my word for it as a veteran of intellectual journalism in New York and Washington—no educated American, apart from members of the creative writing faculties and aspiring poets, pays any attention to contemporary poetry. The reason is that nine-tenths of contemporary poetry is—as Johnson said unjustly of the pastoral—"easy, vulgar and therefore disgusting." The elimination of metrical verse in various forms in favor of arbitrarily-delineated prose ("free verse") has had the unfortunate effect of convincing many people who would have belonged to the audience of poetry in previous eras that they can be poets, too. And they can—if poetry consists of little anecdotes and impressions jotted down in fractured prose.

Silberg criticizes Gioia for favoring formal poets; but here again, Gioia is right. "Formal poetry" is redundant, like "flaming fire." Except for a few experiments, all poetry, in every literary tradition—Greco-Roman, European, Persian, Arabic, Chinese, Indian—was composed in metrical verse, before the early twentieth century. Bad poetry is easy to write and easy to forget; great poetry is hard to write and hard to forget. Great poetry is hard to forget not because of the thoughts or sentiments it expresses (these may well be simple, even banal, like those in Markham's "The Man with the Hoe") or because of its images (which in most poetic traditions have been conventional) but because the use of repeated patterns of sound is a mnemonic device. This is a characteristic of bad verse as well as good verse, of course; but all that means is that genuine poetry has more in common with popular songs, hymns and advertising jingles than it does with the unmusical ramblings of the poseurs and prosateurs who have shaped Silberg's once-modish idea of poetry.

The audience abandoned poetry when poets abandoned verse. Why go to a basketball game or a baseball game, in order to see out-of-shape people mill around aimlessly on the court for a few hours? Until formal poetry and poetry become synonyms again, American poetry will remain as marginal an activity as bird-watching. At least the birds have not forgotten how to sing.

Scott Timberg

An Open Letter to Dana Gioia

4 February, 2001
Los Angeles, CA

Dear Dana Gioia,

I just wanted to tell you how much I enjoyed your "Fallen Western Star" essay—my favorite piece of yours since the original "Can Poetry Matter?" article. The fact that it's breaking some windows up north shows that you're doing your job. Sorry to say, the article reflected much of what I feel about literary life—such as it is—in California.

Down here along the sun-baked freeways of Los Angeles, we're fond of deriding the Bay Area for its pretentiousness, its smug self-importance, its constant need to remind the world of its sophistication and beauty. An editor of mine calls it "boutique city." As it happens, I just spent a few wonderful days in San Francisco and Berkeley. I was amazed at the number of good bookstores and what seemed, to an Angeleno, like a real, living, literary and artistic culture. I saw contemporary music performed in front of a packed house at the Berkeley Symphony Orchestra, haunted used bookstores on Telegraph Avenue, and sat next to a young woman on the bus who was reading with a Latin-English dictionary on her lap. For a few bright midwinter days, the hills and the Bay gleaming, it seemed like paradise. I was reminded, in short, of all the things Northern Californians have to be smug about.

But your essay describes a city increasingly indifferent to living writers even as it names streets for the dead. I wish I could tell you that things were better in your hometown, but I'm afraid that here we are so consumed—as the Eastern, and the San Franciscan, stereotype has it—with Hollywood movies and bad TV. Angelenos in these relatively peaceful post-riot years like to trumpet their city's diversity, and the city is as heterogenous a place as can be imagined. But any community—especially a diverse community—seeks out a common language for communication and connection, and here that common language, so often, is pop culture, and only pop culture. Go to a party or a restaurant, and keep your ears open, if you doubt me.

I can't much compare LA to San Francisco—I've simply not spent enough time up there. But I can certainly say, as a longtime Easterner who's lived and covered the arts in Southern California for almost four years, I've never lived in a place so culturally rich, and where literature was so invisible. I moved to the West Coast from a small port city in Connecticut, where James Merrill was a local hero and where a summer poetry festival drew 2,000 people on a good day. The local shoreline bohemians sponsored readings and put out a gauntlet-throwing literary journal and even published the poetry of New York rock musicians. Before that I was in Chapel Hill, where local literary journals—many with a focus on the New South and its culture—were available in nearly every coffee shop and Algonquin Books keeps Southern writing alive. And here and there I lived in Baltimore, where local fiction writers, too, had status and visibility.

What's funny is that LA is in many ways as pleasing, as sophisticated a place as any of my former haunts. But writers can't get arrested here, despite the fact that California has attracted or produced so many amazing writers—Chandler, Fante, Jeffers, Kael, Didion, Mosley. Their latter-day cousins can't compete with the popular culture that dominates our psychology here, nor connect across the vast distances that Los Angeles shares with other Western cities.

So in some ways, I fear, both cities suffer the same fate. But San Francisco differs from LA in the complacency of its regional life, and this doesn't create the ferment that allows art to grow. (As a kid, it always baffled me that San Francisco bands were so often awful and self-indulgent, like *The Grateful Dead* or *Journey*.) It reminds me of what Auden said about the airy spirit of *The Tempest*. "Ariel, as Shakespeare has told us, has no passions. That is his glory and his limitation. The earthly paradise is a beautiful place, but nothing of serious importance can occur in it."

If San Franciscans have passions these days, they seem to involve money, and the Internet, with fine wine and rustic getaways the rewards—often passionately pursued—for labor in the service of the former. And perhaps it no longer needs to be said that the Internet gang has forced many of the artists and writers out of what we've long been told is America's most deeply bohemian city.

I was especially struck by your suggestion that San Francisco, or perhaps California in general, needs an engaging, contentious, and high-profile critical journal. Ain't that the truth. *The Los Angeles Times Book Review* offers no emphasis on LA or California writers or topics, and has largely ignored local critics; even its crime and detective fiction column, "LA Confidential," is often bereft of Southland writers. While there are a handful of under-the-radar local journals, we don't have anything that compares to *Open City*—a forum for the New York literary avant-garde—or *The Baffler*—the Chicago-based quarterly that mixes Midwestern radicalism and new writing.

Whether it's American Southerners in the 1930s or Scottish vernacular writers in the '90s, authors have always needed local publications—and sometimes, local publishers—to make their mark. As you put it, "A region unable to articulate and advance its native arts will find them ignored in the cultural capitals." Why don't we have a good literary journal or publisher?

San Francisco does have two cultural outlets known to

readers all over the country. The first is *Juxtapoz*, the magazine of the "lowbrow" art movement, which has helped boost the fortunes of car customizers and illustrators who work with hotrod, Catholic, retro '50s, and matchbook iconography. Go to an opening at Hollywood's La Luz de Jesus gallery if you think this magazine is without impact. But it's narrowly focused, and the art it celebrates may not have much staying power.

The wider-ranging and better known San Francisco outlet is *Salon*, the website that once showed a great deal of energy and creativity. But as the Internet has crashed, *Salon* has tightened its coverage, mostly, to sex, technology, and DVDs of films that came out six months ago. The site still does some good work, including its book coverage, but it has no allegiance to California, and it seems appropriate that *Salon*'s literary editor, the very capable Laura Miller, operates out of New York.

As to the root cause of the literary vacuum, I go back and forth. To the Easterner in me, it's not the nice weather and beautiful views, but materialism and superficiality that keeps California from coming up with a serious critical culture. Why invest in something like thinking for its own sake—likely to bring so low a margin on the investment? Especially when there's so much money to be made from movies and computers, or so many hours to put in at the local gym? And criticism—even literature itself—is so much less sexy than talking venture capital in the Silicon Valley, or hanging with starlets on Sunset.

As an Angeleno (and a Palo Alto native, I should add), I blame the insularity of the East. All those self-absorbed New Yorkers writing books about each other in their cramped apartments have kept our culture down. Somewhere between these two poles, I'd wager, is the truth of the matter—and a good literary journal could help us work out exactly where. And start pushing, then, in the right direction.

It's probably not surprising that the most important literary movement among my generational peers—the ironic postmodernists who orbit *McSweeney's*—is based in Brooklyn, the once-derided borough with an active literary scene going back at least to Paul Auster and other writers born in the 1940s.

It seems like poetic justice that much of the gang behind *McSweeney's*, including Dave Eggers (whose success with *A Heartbreaking Work of Staggering Genius* helps finance the whole thing) are Stanford and Berkeley grads. They sharpened their wits with *Might*, the short-lived San Francisco satire magazine of the mid-'90s, before moving East, just as West Coast jazz musicians left California as the '50s ended. (It's worth noting that while the reclusive Eggers recently moved back to San Francisco, his journal and publishing wing continues to be based in New York.)

What do we have in LA that could compete with New York's scene? We sometimes call Silver Lake the Brooklyn of Southern California. But while the neighborhood is full of great thrift shops and cool restaurants—and I'd hold up the café con leche at Café Tropical to anything on Smith Street—it's hard to imagine a literary scene springing from its sweltering pavement. The publications in Silver Lake are about movies, and hipness—those twin California obsessions.

There are many good and some great writers in California, but at least from where I sit, no viable scene or school, besides university campuses—where great art is often appreciated but rarely produced. Because of the lack of an active critical life, and LA's reputation for hype and boosterism, our writers get an indifferent reception elsewhere. In some ways, it's our own damn fault. If we kept high standards and exported only the best literary artists, we'd be taken seriously by New York and London. We could attract and nurture writers with a distinctly local sensibility, writers who could sing of the Golden State's glories and failings. They could give us our own iconography instead of borrowed imagery from 1930s noir, or Eastern stereotypes.

These artists could write for us, and for everyone. What Auden said about poets is, I think, true of artists of all kinds—that they aim to be "like some valley cheese, local, but prized everywhere."

"We Are Not Publishing This in New York"

Jack Foley on *Dancing Bear's Poetry Program*, KKUP, Cupertino 9/13/00

DANCING BEAR: *You seem like a very good person to comment on the "Fallen Western Star Wars" controversy.*

JACK FOLEY: We should perhaps begin one step back from where you might think to begin it—with Dana Gioia's article, "Fallen Western Star." The title of my book *O Powerful Western Star* is taken from Whitman's poem, "When Lilacs Last in the Dooryard Bloom'd." But Whitman actually wrote, "O powerful western *fallen* star!" I deliberately left out the "fallen." Dana Gioia wrote the introduction to *O Powerful Western Star.* I tell people to read the introduction but not to bother with the rest of the book! After he had finished the introduction, Dana had a lot of energy left over, and *The Ruminator Review* (then *The Hungry Mind Review*) asked him to write an essay on this area as a literary region. And he obliged. He wrote a very interesting essay which in fact originated in some of the things he said in the introduction to my book. It's a long essay, and it's called, in reference to my title, "Fallen Western Star." Dana is talking about some problems of this area. That essay came out and I thought it was marvelous, and a lot of people thought it was marvelous, but it also got under the skin of other people. You know how it is if you have an agenda in which you emphasize certain people and feel that this is what it's like here and someone comes along and challenges that. It's not as if Dana is an

77

outsider. He's a Californian, he's a Westerner for heaven's sake! But the people he named as important in current California writing—particularly in Northern California writing—that group of people is different from the group of people that would ordinarily be spoken of by, let's say, Richard Silberg, who didn't like Dana's essay at all. Richard Silberg is a good friend of mine, but we're often at loggerheads aesthetically. (Different strokes for different folks!) Richard wrote an essay attacking Dana's essay; I wrote an essay attacking Richard's essay; Richard answered my attack. Various other people—Howard Junker, Jonah Raskin, David Mason, Jacqueline Marcus, Scott Timberg, Michael Lind—had their say about this as well. These essays will all be published in a book called *The "Fallen Western Star" Wars*. It will be published by Scarlet Tanager Press in Oakland.

DANCING BEAR: Is Scarlet Tanager a West Coast publisher?

JACK FOLEY: Yes! We are not publishing this in New York!

DANCING BEAR: You know, I read this thing as it fell out, so I read Dana's article first and I went, "You know, actually that makes a lot of sense." Then I read Silberg's and I went, "Yeah!" And then I read yours . . .

JACK FOLEY: That isn't what I went when I read Silberg's article. I went "Not yeah" to Silberg's article. A lot of the trouble has to do, I think, with an understanding of what it means to be in the West and whether you like the kinds of conditions that are here. Most of the people who read Dana's article say, "Of course that's true."

DANCING BEAR: If you put it to the backdrop of all the economics that's going on here—everything's moved to New York basically because it's all conglomerated.

JACK FOLEY: As someone at New College said, "I tell my students to publish in New York." There's a lot that's going on here, but the question is really whether it's genuine activity or stuff that's more or less in a vacuum. And this is a problem. It's a problem for a lot of people, not just for me and for Dana. One needs to ask whose work gets featured and talked about as "prominent." Also, the ways in which people talk or do not talk to one another here are certainly problematical. What can be done about all this? Well, one of the things you can do is write articles which stir up a bit of dust—and that happened.

DANCING BEAR: I wanted to ask you one more thing. Going off the premise of what Dana Gioia wrote in his essay and what you followed up on, in that there is no real, serious publishing of literature going on in the West Coast the way it is in New York—where you would expect it to be a major hub of activity—if you look at the Internet, where a lot of publishers are going online, I see a sense of community there where I don't see it at times in the physical world here.

JACK FOLEY: You know, I go to a lot of readings and I've put on a lot of events. These things begin to build some community. That's certainly true: there is a poetry community of people who know each other. The question is whether this community is genuinely vital, whether something is happening here, as it certainly did happen when the Beats were here and in fact before the Beats, with the "Berkeley Renaissance," which involved Robert Duncan and Jack Spicer and others. That pre-dated the Beats. Something was afoot then. Something was also afoot in the seventies when the L=A=N=G=U=A=G=E poets were happening. What's afoot now?

DANCING BEAR: I correspond a lot with writers on the net. I've never met them, yet we share ideas and talk about things—poetics and all sorts of things—and I almost feel as if the Internet then becomes the next big "Powerful Star," a community.

JACK FOLEY: Well, I think that there is a difference, that there are things that happen in the poetry reading that you can't get anywhere else. One of the principal effects of just about every modern "convenience" has been to isolate people in their houses. Insofar as we're communicating with people on the Internet— and I do it too—we are disembodied. One of the things we need to remember is that human existence is to some degree always local and from the body. A poetry reading is one of the few places where we can actually physically connect with an artist. We have this funny relationship to people we don't know, can't know, and who may well have no conception of us at all: movie stars, rock stars, whatever. We may fall in love with them. Ivan Argüelles wrote a long poem, *Madonna Septet*, about an obsession with the pop star Madonna, whom he's never met, doesn't know in any way, will never meet. We have these deep feelings for these people we don't know and who don't know us. And that is, on the one hand, wonderful in some ways, but in other ways, as Jimmy Durante used to say, it's a catasterstroke. It's distressing and awful in other ways. The physical aspect of people—bodies, just bodies connecting—is something one can find at a poetry reading. So both of these things are true. Yes, the Internet is a kind of community, but there are also aspects to a physical community which you ain't gonna get from the Internet.

DANCING BEAR: *That's true. I hadn't thought of that part.*

JACK FOLEY: It's important, I think—especially when people start talking about poetry that's written from the body. My wife Adelle and I perform, and there are certain things that happen in a performance which will be different from what happens in film, in video, on radio. It's a different kind of experience. The fact that we're all breathing the same air, that we're physically present to one another, makes a difference—it's something that can be exploited by your performance. The "Fallen Western Star Wars" dispute raises the question of exactly what sort of specific locality we have here—which is an important question—but it also raises the question of what constitutes a locality.

Jack Foley

CODA

The purpose of this essay has not been to
answer questions but to raise them. . . .
    —Dana Gioia, "Fallen Western Star"

It seems to me that there is something genuinely new in Dana Gioia's perceptions about the San Francisco Bay Area literary scene. But perhaps the new never manifests without someone complaining that it is not the old. Thus this debate!

I want to end this piece about a literary quarrel with two quotations.

The first is from the much-argued-about Charles Edwin Markham: lines from a poem, "A Lyric of the Dawn," which scarcely anyone reads anymore. The poem appeared in Markham's first book, *The Man with the Hoe and Other Poems* (1899). I find the lines odd, old-fashioned, Shelleyan, mournful, gorgeous:

> Alone I list
>   In the leafy tryst;
> Silent the woodlands in their starry sleep—
> Silent the phantom wood in waters deep:
> No footfall of a wind along the pass
> Startles a harebell—stirs a blade of grass.
>   Yonder the wandering weeds,

Enchanted in the light,
Stand in the gusty hollows, still and white...

Sing out, O throstle, sing:
I follow on, my king:
Lead me forever through the crimson dawn—
Till the world ends, lead me on!
Ho there! He shouts again—he sways—and now,
Upspringing from the bough,
Flashing a glint of dew upon the ground,
Without a sound
He drops into a valley and is gone!

It is sometimes forgotten that Markham did not remain in California after the success of "The Man with the Hoe." Like many a Californian, he packed his bags and headed for New York, where, in 1940, he died. The *Encyclopaedia Britannica* remarks that Markham's later volumes "have the commanding rhetoric but lack the passion of the early works."

The second quotation is from W.H. Auden. Auden was writing in 1949 about California native (born in Oakland) Rosalie Moore; Moore was a member of a now almost entirely forgotten California group called "The Activists," which at the time regarded itself as in competition with the Beats. "In conclusion," writes Auden,

> may I suggest to the reader, whatever his preferences in poetry, not that he should be tolerant of opposing views in the sense of ceasing to hold any, but that, as a lover of poetry, he should be glad that oppositions exist, for poetry flourishes when the opponents are determined and evenly matched but, if any party gains too complete a victory and succeeds in suppressing its rivals, poetry invariably declines.

Soit. The fury of language which is poetry becomes, sometimes, another sort of fury, a mode of opposition which may be the prelude to growth.

CONTRIBUTORS

Editor *Jack Foley*'s most recent books are the companion critical volumes *O Powerful Western Star* (recipient of the Artists Embassy Literary/Cultural Award 1998-2000) and *Foley's Books: California Rebels, Beats, and Radicals*. Among his poetry books are *Exiles, Adrift,* and *Gershwin*. Foley's radio show, "Cover to Cover," is heard every Wednesday on Berkeley station KPFA; his column, "Foley's Books," appears weekly in the online magazine *The Alsop Review* (www.alsopreview.com). He is a Contributing Editor of *Poetry Flash*. For the past thirty-seven years he has lived in Oakland, California.

Dana Gioia was born in Los Angeles. He received his B.A. and M.B.A. from Stanford University. He also completed an M.A. at Harvard where he studied with poets Robert Fitzgerald and Elizabeth Bishop. Gioia is the author of *Can Poetry Matter?: Essays on Poetry and American Culture* as well as three collections of poetry, *Interrogations at Noon, The Gods of Winter* and *Daily Horoscope,* and *Nosferatu,* a libretto. He lives in Santa Rosa, California.

Howard Junker founded ZYZZYVA, the journal of West Coast writers and artists, in 1985 and has edited four anthologies of work taken from its pages, most recently *Lucky Break: How I Became a Writer* (Heinemann). He has contributed to a number of magazines, including *Architectural Digest, Art in America,*

Artforum, ARTS, Connoisseur, Esquire, Film Comment, Film Quarterly, Harper's Bazaar, The Nation, The New Republic, New York, Playboy, Rolling Stone, The Village Voice, and *Vogue*. In the late sixties he was an associate editor of *Newsweek*, writing about art, books, movies, and theater.

Michael Lind, a Senior Fellow at the New America Foundation and a Lecturer at Harvard Law School, is the best-selling author of a number of books, including *The Next American Nation* (The Free Press, 1995), *Vietnam* (The Free Press, 1999), and a novel, *Powertown* (Harpercollins, 1996). His poems and criticism have appeared in *Poetry, Partisan Review, The Hudson Review*, and other journals. His books of verse include a narrative poem, *The Alamo* (Houghton Mifflin, 1997), a children's book in verse, *Bluebonnet Girl* (Henry Holt, 2001) and a collection of lyric poems, *When You Are Someone Else* (Aralia Press, 2001).

David Mason's books include *The Buried Houses, The Country I Remember*, and *The Poetry of Life and the Life of Poetry*, from Story Line Press. With Mark Jarman he co-edited *Rebel Angels: 25 Poets of the New Formalism*, and with the late John Frederick Nims he co-edited the 4th edition of *Western Wind: An Introduction to Poetry*. He teaches at The Colorado College, and lives in the mountains outside Colorado Springs.

Jacqueline Marcus's first book of poems, *Close to the Shore*, will be published by Michigan State University Press in the spring of 2002. Her poems have appeared in *The Kenyon Review, The Antioch Review, The Wallace Stevens Journal, The Journal, Poetry International, The Ohio Review, The Literary Review* and elsewhere. New poems appear in *Faultline, Poet Lore* and at the e-journal, *Exquisite Corpse*. Jacqueline Marcus is the editor of *ForPoetry.com*. She teaches philosophy at Cuesta College.

Jonah Raskin is the chair of the communication studies department at Sonoma State University and the author of six books, including *Out of the Whale, The Mythology of Imperialism*, and *For the Hell of It: The Life and Times of Abbie Hoffman*.

He is a poet, a performance artist, and the book reviewer for the *Santa Rosa Press Democrat*. He is now writing a biography of Allen Ginsberg.

Richard Silberg is Associate Editor of *Poetry Flash* and co-director of *"Poetry Flash* at Cody's." His social philosophy book, *The Devolution of the People* was published by Harcourt, Brace & World in 1967. His books of poetry include *Translucent Gears, The Fields, Totem Pole,* and *Doubleness*, which was published in the California Poetry Series. *Reading the Sphere*, essays from *Poetry Flash*, is forthcoming.

Scott Timberg was born in the San Francisco Bay Area in 1969, and educated at Wesleyan University and the University of North Carolina at Chapel Hill. He covers Southern California's arts and popular culture for *New Times Los Angeles*, a weekly, and has also contributed to *The Baltimore Sun*, the *Boston Phoenix*, *GQ*, and *The SF Weekly*. He lives in Los Angeles.

Also from Scarlet Tanager Books:

Wild One by Lucille Lang Day
poetry, 100 pages, $12.95

Catching the Bullet & Other Stories by Daniel Hawkes
fiction, 64 pages, $12.95

Visions: Paintings Seen Through the Optic of Poetry
by Marc Elihu Hofstadter
poetry, 72 pages, $14.00

red clay is talking by Naomi Ruth Lowinsky
poetry, 142 pages, $14.95

Everything Irish by Judy Wells
poetry, 112 pages, $12.95